Praise for To Call M

A beautifully written, gripping account ... This book reminded me of Yalom's writing about therapy – once I started reading it I really couldn't put it down."

Therapy Today

I cannot recommend this book highly enough... It is an important book in the context of the discipline and practice of psychotherapy and will be of use to clients, trainees, trainers and therapist.

British Journal of Guidance & Counselling

An interesting and enjoyable read for therapists at all levels of training, for clients (or potential clients), and for the general reader because of the insight it gives into what really happens in therapy, or in one particular therapy, with two unique individuals

Private Practice

Engaging and powerful ... a breathtaking account ... A lovely book, a rose with all its thorns and a full-bodied fragrance. Highly recommended!

Psychosynthesis Quarterly

A gift to the reader... I recommend this book to anyone interested in understanding how individual and group therapy can heal. It may be of special interest to those of us who also seek to accompany our clients imaginatively in their ongoing search for their true selves.

Irish Council for Psychotherapy Newsletter

It is no easy matter to convey the sense of a psychoanalytic session, but McHugh does this with great success.

Irish Independent

'Probably one of the best books I've ever read about therapy and the process of therapy. If you liked *In Treatment* you will absolutely love this book. It's powerful, absolutely beautifully written ... spectacularly well written ... jawdroppingly good.'

Peter Sheridan's review on *RTE Liveline*

TO CALL MYSELF
BELOVED

Eina McHugh

NEW ISLAND

To Call Myself Beloved
First published 2012
by New Island
2 Brookside
Dundrum Road
Dublin 14

www.newisland.ie

Copyright © Eina McHugh, 2012
The author has asserted her moral rights.

PRINT ISBN   :   978-1-84840-184-6
EPUB ISBN   :   978-1-84840-185-2
MOBI ISBN   :   978-1-84840-186-0

All rights reserved. The material in this publication is protected
by copyright law. Except as may be permitted by law, no part of
the material may be reproduced (including by storage in a retrieval
system) or transmitted in any form or by any means; adapted;
rented or lent without the written permission of the copyright
owner.

British Library Cataloguing Data. A CIP catalogue record for this
book is available from the British Library

Typeset by JM InfoTech INDIA
Cover design by Nina Lyons
Printed by Bell & Bain Ltd, Glasgow

New Island received financial assistance from The Arts Council
(An Comhairle Ealaíon), Dublin, Ireland

10 9 8 7 6 5 4 3 2 1

For Nan and Brendan, with love

Man's spiritual development is a long and arduous journey, an adventure through strange lands full of surprises, difficulties and even dangers.

Roberto Assagioli, *Psychosynthesis: A Manual of Principles and Techniques* (1975)

At the end of the analysis, it can happen that neither the analyst nor the patient knows exactly what happened. There's a story about the analyst Annie Reich, who once described a very good analysis at a conference. People were impressed, and said, 'You should write up this analysis,' and she said, 'I'm not ready to write about it, because I haven't yet figured out what happened.' The analysis had been finished for several years, and she still hadn't figured it out.

Janet Malcolm, *Psychoanalysis: The Impossible Profession* (2004)

Contents

I

Beginnings

But often, in the world's most crowded streets,
But often, in the din of strife,
There rises an unspeakable desire
After the knowledge of our buried life;
A thirst to spend our fire and restless force
In tracking out our true, original course;

Matthew Arnold, 'The Buried Life'

I AM eyeing the fraying psychoanalytic couch, the like of which I have previously seen only in foreign documentaries and Woody Allen films. Thanks be to God we are sitting opposite each other in ordinary armchairs.

J is not how I imagined him. Phil, my friend, had been a student on one of his courses. When I was sick in bed, with that same dull body ache I could not shrug off for months, she had suggested that I talk to him. 'You know, he's excellent. I felt safe with him. I'd trust him. Anyway,' she added cheerfully, as if this was the crucial criterion in choosing a psychotherapist, 'he's awfully good-looking.'

And she is right: he is, but not in the bespectacled, bearded, stereotypical way I had expected. J is a clear-eyed, clean-shaven man. Well dressed – formal three-piece suit, no less – he looks youngish, maybe late thirties, with a presence that seems older and almost steely still. Now he is asking a reasonable question – 'What brings you here?' – and coolly awaiting a reply. Only I do not know what to say. I want to project an articulate confidence, for that is what I do, no matter how it feels inside. I do not know how to reveal the baffling problems that have led me to his door. Work is the easiest way to tiptoe into the process.

'Work seems to be all of me. I'm managing an innovative media-training project that hasn't been properly set up. I seem to spend hours travelling, looking for a solution to endless crises. Only I don't think there is one.'

I probably did not say that; this is what my imagination remembers.

Implacable gaze back.

'How old are you?'

'Twenty-seven.'

Does J ask more about my age to elicit details? I tell him that I studied and worked in Dublin until I took up this job two years ago, in the autumn of 1986. It is the first time I have lived in Belfast, although, as he can detect from my accent, I am Northern Irish. I miss my friends from Dublin terribly.

'Sexual relationships?'

Maybe he does not ask that; it is just understood that other kinds of relationships are possible.

'I'm single. Relationships are ... well ... they're ...'

Try to find the word, any old word will do. How to tell him that I've never had a sexual relationship, that the very thought of it fills me with queasy anxiety? How to tell him that this is probably why I'm really here, to make sense of the sick-making fear that is such a frightening mystery? The whole mix-up of how I don't want a sexual relationship. I have my friends – that's my form of loving, and yet, and yet, I can't seem to cross over into woman-hood and sexuality. And it is a vicious circle because I've no experience, and something has to be done in a sexual relationship, but I don't know – rising panic – what it is. I'm not like other people, the way they enjoy relation-ships, the way they're *good* at them, seem to know what to do. Yet all this is beyond intelligible language, so round and round I go in an enclosed mind circuit.

Silence from him – not necessarily cold.

Let's go back to talking about work, for I love work. That media course after college led to me developing an arts and communications initiative for young people at risk. The project had been creatively satisfying until a peculiar feeling had taken over, as if I could not figure out where they stopped and I began, could not discern who or what was at risk. The problem, I am sure, is my workaholic personality.

'Tell me about your family.'

I am sketching a snapshot in brush strokes: 'Both my parents are alive. I don't see much of them. I don't know why. They'd love to see more of me. My father: he's a wonderful man. My mother and I ... we're not that close. I live with my aunt – my mother's sister. I've a clever sister who is two years older than me; she lives in London. I've two brothers: one's a year older, the other several years younger. The thing is I don't see much of any of them.'

The disconcerting realisation is descending that few aspects of my life feel good. It is hard to judge what J is thinking: his impassive face gives no clues. He asks intelligent questions, seeks clarification, occasionally glancing down, making minuscule gestures as though clearing fluff from his suit. It is odd to hear myself sharing intimacies with a stranger, even if he is a professional psychotherapist.

However, there is one question to which I have no reply. I have found myself drawn to telling him about a rootless childhood. The first moving around was in England, where I was born. My Irish father and Northern Irish mother had returned to rural Northern Ireland in 1967, when I was six, immediately before the 'Troubles' started. My parents wanted to bring up their children in Ireland. They used every penny of their savings to build their dream house in a politically tense village, near the border with the Republic.

'The house was opposite a police station. They thought it would keep us safe. They didn't know what was coming.'

He is Northern Irish and will understand the code: danger. I have already sussed – from his first name, the minute giveaways that are implicit in any Northern Irish conversation – that he is a Catholic, like me.

'There was always trouble in the town. Our house was bombed several times. We got caught up in it all. Each time we moved away, but came back again.'

He listens and lets the space between us be. Then he asks, in a strikingly slow, careful voice, 'Why did you keep going back to danger? Why didn't you move to safety?'

It is years – if ever – since I have spoken about this, although memories have been shifting over the past three months, through weekly meetings with a male counsellor. There is a silver thread in the maze of the unconscious I am unravelling. I know there is an answer to J's question. There has got to be one, but, for the life of me, I don't know what it is. No one has asked me such a direct, almost obvious, question. He is waiting, looking with those steady eyes, not interjecting in order to close an uncomfortable gap. I offer a superficial response, and we move on to another subject, but the lack of a satisfactory answer echoes uneasily inside.

'Why do you want to work with me?'

I hear myself say something surprising: 'I want you to confront me.' I have already formed the fantasy that he is tough, capable, can handle me. He says that he combines two trainings, one in psychoanalysis, the other in psychosynthesis, and uses an impressive phrase to describe his approach: bifocal vision. I nod nonchalantly, the way I do when I haven't got a clue what the other person is saying. He explains that he uses the couch in his practice – an airy wave of the hand indicating the dormant beast on my right, his tone an unspoken 'It's non-negotiable.'

Nervous tummy flutters.

I want to impress him with my eager diligence. 'I'm prepared to do whatever's needed. You know, like reading or doing homework.'

Does one do homework in psychoanalysis? Oh well, it sounds good, and these are my traditional coping strategies: work, work, work.

A challenging reply: 'She doth protest too much, methinks.'

Christ, he is decidedly odd. The conversation turns to the unusual fact that I have registered for a weekend workshop with him in two days' time. I had booked it weeks earlier, loving the poetry of the description: 'Psychosynthesis: A Psychology of Soul'.

'Why don't you see how the weekend goes?'

The exploratory meeting is drawing to a close when I decide to speak bluntly: 'You don't seem in the slightest bit interested.'

That smooth face does not react – perhaps a quizzical arch of an eyebrow, not a flicker more. I seem to remember his laconic reply, 'Now you have two men willing to work with you.' He was referring to himself and the counsellor I had been seeing. That must mean he was willing to take me on. 'I must stop. Let me help you with your coat.'

Out I go. What an unnerving meeting. What a curious man.

There were things I did not tell J that day. I did not disclose that over the previous eleven months I had lost nearly three and a half stone, revealing to the world a fragile body which had been hiding beneath protective layers of fat. And everything was changing: the shape of my face, my hair, even my eyes – the glasses I had worn since my teenage years had been replaced with the exhilarating freedom of contact lenses.

I did not tell J that a few weeks previously I had taken part in a Jungian workshop, during which there been a meditation on a bowl and a sword. The bowl I had drawn was an ugly relic of a vessel – untouched, unloved and abandoned. Only faintly underneath the cobwebs could be discerned sensual pink and purple Celtic spirals, a lost world of beauty waiting to be unearthed. Next to the bowl I had drawn blue water, like an undulating sea: the water the bowl needed to wash away the dust.

Afterwards I had talked with the woman leading the weekend, a therapist from England. I was crying, which was rare. I could not stop the swelling grief, sensing that the image related to my own wounded relationship with the feminine. 'Where does the water come from?' she had asked, pointing to the sea. The thing was, I could not reply. 'Could the water be your tears?' she suggested, and at that I felt moved.

Finally, I did not tell J that I had been thinking about a line from E.M. Forster's *Howards End* for months. To mention it would be plain ridiculous, yet the same refrain kept reverberating: 'only connect...'.

That night, my bedroom lit up with a dream. I was with a big man, my darling Daddy. I was standing there before him, crying inconsolably, as only a child can. You see, I was asking him the therapist's question, yet, through the torrent of tears, only one jagged ache of a word could emerge: why? Now an outer sound was crashing in. It took a few dazed seconds of semi-waking before the realisation dawned that the sobbing was no longer confined to the dream space; it was emanating from me. I hushed myself, but the body, which had always seemed a far-off object, would not be silenced until it was ready. Gradually the shaking subsided, and I was left alone, with a powerful sense of shock, sorrow and sadness.

I did not understand what this was about. All I knew was that it was connected to meeting the therapist. A submerged part of me had been called out. The therapist and I had clicked, and this click was not related to liking or loathing each other; it was based on some other, deeper communication. He had whispered to my unconscious, and my unconscious had responded with a stunning dream. He had called me in. Maybe it was the other way around; maybe it was both. My inner world had awakened. He was the one for me.

When the psychosynthesis weekend started two days later, it was as if its teachings were calling me back to some inner home I had never known existed yet immediately recognised to be true. Psychosynthesis, I heard J explain, was a holistic psychology. *Psyche* was the Greek word for soul – he spoke with passionate commitment – and *synthesis* meant that drive towards wholeness. Human beings, he said, were essentially spiritual beings, embodied on an unfolding journey of discovery. Then he said, 'You are not your feelings.' The phrase danced around. What could he mean?

'Depression can be frozen anger turned inwards,' he added – another intriguing idea. 'There is nothing frightening in yourself. All internal monsters have an energy that can be transformed in inner dialogue.'

His musical phrases rolled over the room.

'The pull of the psyche is towards organic wholeness.'

'Whatever is underdeveloped or expelled from consciousness will seek to return, like a boomerang.'

'The return of the repressed can be disguised in the form of a symptom.'

'Creative disorder can be something new trying to emerge.'

'Crisis, in Chinese, means the exciting potential of opportunity.'

Reflecting on my relationship to feelings, I revealed the until-now unconscious pact I had made that anything experienced as negative, such as sadness or anger, must be denied. Happiness was to be ruthlessly promoted by my mind. In response to the question 'What are your significant activities?' one motif was incessantly repeated: work. *I feel dominated and driven by work. The crashing highs and lows. The constant desire for admiration. The obsessive perfection. The need for control and brilliance. Work enlivens and depresses me.*

In response to the invitation to complete the sentence, 'My life is like …' I had written in a tired scrawl: *My life is like space, filled with satellites and planets. The planets are out there somewhere – revolving, unconnected, wandering, empty, eerie, threatening.*

J was a superb teacher, leading the group not necessarily with effusiveness but with an incisive and, yes, deliberately provocative style. In how he responded to people, he seemed to know something of pain and joy, suffering and confusion. He knew his stuff, exuded a professional confidence, suffused with intelligent compassion. I sensed that he had walked the long stony territory himself, which made me feel secure. And he had a quirky, teasing sense of humour. I liked him, trusted him and enjoyed him.

I felt a physical surge of faith, a conviction, a knowing. He might not take me on, but I had to try. I thought he could help me. I also sensed that, if I was to set out on a psychoanalytically based therapy, I would have to squirrel away those glimpses of a good-hearted guide; if I worked with him, the shutters of his self would remain closed at times, as they had seemed in our first meeting.

I would not have stayed the course of therapy without that introductory weekend. Counselling was no longer my path, yet it had played the invaluable role of getting me started.

'Why should I take you on?'

I was in his room again. The message was clear. He was very busy, with many patients. There was no guarantee of a space. The personal warmth of the weekend had evaporated; his other, cordoned-off self was back. Maybe I misunderstood his question, believing that he wanted me to lobby my case over the others who needed him. Should I declare, 'Look, I'm your ultimate patient, the one who'll inspire you,' which, of course, I already narcissistically yearned to be. I could line up my problems like tantalising sweeties. However, buoyed up by the weekend's emphasis on choosing, rather than compulsively reacting, I defiantly replied, 'I've made my choice. Your choice is up to you.'

When he spoke next, it was the first of many times when I could hear that hint of barely concealed exasperation which would later rise up into undulations of full-scale, outright irritation as we engaged in that grand therapeutic undertaking, a right old barney. Perhaps from the outset the knowledge was there that aspects of me annoyed him, and vice versa. Eventually he let the question go and moved on to set out his terms. He did not see anyone less often than once a week because the work required that level of contact. I replied, 'I think I'll need to come along at least twice a week.' The words seemed to have a driving force, a will, almost outside of me.

There was the money: £20 a session, £40 a week. I would have to have such faith in my earning abilities in a volatile world of short-term projects.

Yes.

And the contract? I was to turn up, speak whatever was in my mind and pay.

Yes.

Then there were my needs. Well, I had read a little of these matters and thought it best to pitch in with a thing or two. I stressed I could see him only for as long as I had the money. So how many months would it take?

'It is not possible to know that now. Each person is different. Some people come along and six months is enough. Other people have been working with me for three years.'

An unthinkable swathe of time stretched out ahead. I would be ancient, and broke. There was trusting encouragement in his voice. 'Things will take their course. We begin, and the way will unfold.'

I often wonder what would have happened if, at that moment, a mythical messenger had appeared and revealed the events that would come to pass. I would have been immensely intimidated and would have turned back. But naivety is a valuable commodity in psychotherapy. It propels you forward, and the process itself strengthens resources you never knew you had and offers unexpected gifts in the darkest hours.

'OK.'

I would have to be one of those bargain-basement six-month people, wouldn't I?

The negotiations turned to time. Was it possible to meet in the evenings because I was not sure if I could get out of work during the day? He told me there was a waiting list for evenings. Could I be added? He nodded.

The fact was he had no regular free time over the next few weeks. We would have to go along with whatever haphazard hours he could make available. It was the first indicator that it would take shared effort and goodwill, a joint pulling together, to make this thing work. We would see how we got on for six 'sessions' – a new acorn for my linguistic store – and after that we would review the situation.

Agreed.

He was endorsing my courage in entering therapy, reframing it from an act of middle-class self-indulgence – how most of the media described it – to a heroic venture. I was grappling with difficulties, and these difficulties had repercussions for me, and for others. To attempt to understand them, to take responsibility, was an act of citizenship. He was invoking an uplifting context for our work, and the beauty of his words inspired my soul.

He was taking me on.

'Thank you.'

I thought we could go on talking about therapy in general and keep at bay the dreaded couch lurking to my right. He was changing gear, gesturing brightly towards the you-know-what.

'Well, we've twenty minutes left. Why don't you start on the couch?'

I was stunned. 'What? You mean now?'

Silent scrutiny of eyes. Perhaps this was his strategy to help patients cross over into this unconventional land. If so, it was a clever one, because his manner conveyed everyday business in a setting he obviously loved. Every fantasy was being dredged up – what fearful unknown awaited me?

We both stood facing each other. His right hand extended to the object graciously sheltering against the wall, not squashy and plump like a friendly sofa but a genuine, worn psychoanalyst's couch.

I gingerly lowered myself onto its edge, wondering what on earth to do. He had gone to sit in the equally worn armchair behind the couch. The disembodied voice was helpful.

'You can take off your shoes. Make yourself com-fortable.'

It was so bizarre, like being in a Japanese teahouse with age-old ceremonies about which I knew nothing.

Gripping silence. What happens now?

Then – how marvellous – a bridging question, offered with a relaxed sense of grace. 'Tell me some more about your family.'

We had begun.

In November 1988, the Yellow Pages telephone directory announced a total of three psychotherapists in Belfast.

The dank, sour smell of the 'Troubles' slunk in every alley-way, slyly infiltrating clothes, hair and skin. Bored security men frisked bags in shop entrances. Sectarian murders and relatives' pleas for no reprisals were reported on the evening news. By 6.30 p.m., the city centre was a deserted ghost town. I never noticed it. It was home. Yet now I had the novelty of therapy.

In the early weeks, I would take whatever time he had going. Once he rang me with that courteous formality I was coming to recognise. 'I have had a very late cancel-lation for the next session. I know this is short notice ...' 'I'll come,' I replied. I put on my coat and said to my colleagues, 'I'm stepping out for an early lunch.' A week later, I had two sessions on the same day, something that never happened again. We were manoeuvring around his busy diary as I waited for the ultimate accolade: the allo-cation of my own sacred time.

Undertaking therapy presented me with a crucial question about my relationship with work: how could I take two hours a week out of my schedule for myself? What would I tell my colleagues? The act of making time and money available had major psychological repercus-sions. I had to find the inner authority to put my own needs first, to acknowledge that I *had* needs.

Whenever I had an appointment with J, I would leave the office at exactly twelve minutes to the hour. I had learned that it did not serve to go earlier because he had another patient and I would be intruding on their sanctu-ary by buzzing the bell. The art was to gauge it perfectly, to get there as soon as the previous patient had left, but not be late, for every second mattered.

His name on the intercom was faded, like the build-ing itself.

Buzz.

Pause.

Buzz.

The stiff front door would crank open. On the ground floor, to the left, was a hairdresser's, not glitzy or glam, just 'cut your hair, love', in a halfway-decent style, for less than a tenner. On the right was a wholesale clothes shop where a dark-skinned man used to look out, then glance away, bored, when he saw it was that same young woman again. Straight ahead was a rickety old-fashioned lift, a cupboard into which you could step, pull over the concertina grating and shudder to the top floor. I liked to bound up the stairs, up, up, past the solicitor's office, up to the door where I would knock and wait, until out he would come.

The building made me feel safe. I loved that psycho-therapy had a place alongside getting your hair blow-dried and sorting out a will. It was not necessarily an esoteric world. And later, when an internal craziness seemed to have been unleashed, I would walk down the stairs, feeling the comfort of an ordinary life, of which psycho-therapy was a part for me.

I was always anxious that I might meet someone I knew on the staircase. This was the North, where con-nections were enmeshed into one close-knit web. The truth was I was deeply ashamed of going to J's office. Yet I was also curious about the people I occasionally passed on the stairs because they looked much older than me. My hope was that I was his youngest client – sorry,

patient (from the Latin, *patior*, to suffer) – for J was teaching me about the process of therapy. I longed for the
support of a fellow patient, someone who could relate to
the analytical experience. There was only ever a nod, the
sole acknowledgement that you come here too.

The door would open, and there he would be,
dependable and reliable, ever immaculately dressed. It
was becoming normal: taking off my coat, walking over
to the couch, sliding off my shoes, lying back with my
legs outstretched, speaking into what first felt like nothingness, a rambling to myself, only to realise, when a low
sound would rumble, *Gosh, there's someone else here.* Within
the opening weeks he was mapping out a mosaic of words
that I, apparently, kept unconsciously repeating.

Shattered. Betrayed. Safe. Special. After a while, I got
the hang of it and noticed an expression I used a lot: 'bits
and pieces'.

'I'm in bits and pieces.'

The conversation could start anywhere: a saved-up
office incident, something that had happened over the
weekend, a comment he had made during the previous
session and which I had been mulling over. There was the
freedom of someone being paid to listen to me – sheer
heaven! – even though he said little, offering prompts that
were distinctive and thought-provoking. Mostly there was
the experience of being listened to in silence, very different from the half-hearted attempts that pass for listening
in society. Even odder was listening to myself, for there
was so much quiet, waiting and stillness, a symphony
of breaths, a powerful rocking, a lulling, a pulling back
through form and space, back, back, in and under the

lapping of the conscious mind, to earlier times. It was the sounds that I liked: the sing-song vowels, his and mine. I was being eased into this universe of the unconscious, with its dreams and repetitions, which could be carriers of meaning – of what I did not yet know – mingled with J's free-flowing references to myths and stories.

At the end of six sessions I had no doubt: I wanted to go on. I had found the experience helpful. His was the cautious presence I was coming to know.

'Let's take our time to think about this together,' J suggested.

January 1989. Roll of the drums, fanfare of trumpets. I am the proud possessor of two regular weekly sessions; 10 a.m. on Mondays and 2 p.m. on Wednesdays. The problem is I have to be in Dublin or London on four occasions over the next month. When I casually tell him, assuming that our appointments can be rearranged ('For heaven's sake, it's work. What can I do?'), his face is like granite. There is a distinct chill of severity. This is the pivotal moment of commitment, the moment I think occurs in every serious therapy, when the fundamental question has to be faced: are you in or out? Psychotherapy is a tremendous act of will, requiring determination and persistence to see it through.

A few days later, I returned. 'Look, I can come along.' He never knew of the wrangling I had had to undergo with my boss. Later there was bitterness when he suggested that I was rigid, that therapy with him now meant too much to me. I replied furiously, 'You asked for a commitment and I gave it.' And later again we learned to work around each other, allowing flexibility into a more mature relationship. However, these were the early weeks when two sets of the unconscious needed to synchronise.

A small, significant event seemed to be a good omen. A colleague had unexpectedly arrived from London to discuss a possible project and wanted to meet me at the same time as one of the newly allocated sessions. I felt guilty but, after soul-searching, nominated another team member to take my place. After the session, I went to catch the train to Dublin. There, at the ticket counter, was the visitor. 'Are you on the same train?' I was, and the journey was spent happily developing the project.

You see, I had decided the gods would look after me if I kept faith with the process. Nothing would be lost by taking two hours a week out of work, whereas some insight that could make a difference to my entire life might be missed by not attending those two sessions.

There was the shock and delight that J remembered my story. How did he recall everything, because he did not seem to take notes? Yet he remembered not simply the name of my friend, or the town I went to school in, but also slipped in minute references as if he knew the fabric of my being intimately. He was like a still-life painter, attending to the strawberry in the bowl of fruit, knowing that it was in the detail that the painting would be brought alive.

I am telling J about my older sister, extolling her prodigious talent, explaining how she was the first person from school to win a place at Cambridge, how she writes for swish magazines, how she is single like me. Like all four children.

He utters an extraordinary thing. 'I am interested in *you.*'

'You' is articulated with chiselled emphasis. He must not understand. This is a fascinating story, for my sister is gifted, and am I not supposed to keep him interested? I know he encourages, 'Say what's in your mind,' but I want to package witty stories to keep him entertained. When he hears more, he too will be drawn into the glittering world of the brilliant sister. I embark again on my eulogy, in whose voice (my own? another's?) I do not know. She sings, does Irish dancing, wins the medals I covet, although sometimes we dance together, the two sisters doing their jig. My father adores her. Everyone says they are inseparable. She gets on *so* well with my mother.

Sometimes I have to concentrate to catch his every word.

'I am not interested in her. I am interested in ...' – *pause* – 'you. *You* are the one who interests me.'

'You' fills the room with its knockout punch. He wants to know *me. I* interest him. Warmth and sadness enter my heart. I surrender to my first experience of crying in shared space. Trust is growing between us. The endless straining to be clever can be suspended as J's words tuck over me like a blanket. And there is the first dawning in consciousness of how I have felt about myself and the sister complex for time eternal. The speaking can start again when I am ready, and maybe I can reply to his sensitively paced question, 'What are the tearful thoughts?'

J is curious about my problems, actively engaged in the mutual adventure of analytical enquiry. He wants to create space for the symptoms, to let them breathe a while, with no demand for instant resolution.

'You don't have to make sense here,' he assures me, a glorious relief. His open energy is infectious. A thought constellates: maybe I could be interested in me too. I don't have to keep on terrorising myself with the punishing thought: that there's something wrong with me.

Early on he asks quietly, 'Are you a virgin?'

From the safety of the couch I think, my God, what a shockingly brave question – one the other counsellor had never asked. I am taken aback, not used to talking about this with anyone, never mind a man. It makes me think: yes, he really does mean it when he keeps reiterating that we can talk about private matters here, include unspeakable secrets or painful things that I cannot tell other people. Hope is rising. If he is able to broach these matters – cleanly, honestly – to assign straightforward language to the sexual, then perhaps I can respond. I realise from his question that he does not understand the extent of my inexperience.

I summon up the courage. 'Yes.' Try to explain. What is the explanation? 'The thing is ...' Go on, tell him. 'I've never had a boyfriend. Actually ...' It feels like I'm confessing murder, 'I've never kissed anyone.' My secret is out. My voice is trailing, but he is listening, I know he is. 'No, I can't manage that kind of relationship. Honestly, I'm hopeless.'

Talking about a sexual relationship felt like planning a trip to one of those magical planets beyond Mars; it would never happen anyway, so what was the point of taking the notion seriously?

I was sorry that I could not help J do his job properly. If I had already been in a relationship, there might be significant incidents to explore. I would have something literal, something physical, to offer him; but there was nothing, nothing at all. This dilemma in therapy precisely mirrored my problem in the external world.

'I couldn't have a se- ... se- ... se- ...' – it was hard to get that word out – 'sexual relationship.' The reason was obvious, why did I need to add more? J seemed genuinely interested. 'Because ... you see ... and then ...' My syllables were slipping down the crevices of anxiety. J retrieved them before they disappeared.

'You are not finishing your sentences again.'

I had not noticed this, caught up in my own agitation.

'I've nothing to offer a man. I don't know what to do with a man.'

For one second, a gash was exposed which seemed to run through the whole of my being. It was too excruciating to touch. It needed evasive cloudiness as protection. I hoped he had grasped enough now, that it would all disappear through faith in therapy.

It was such a cruel Catch-22. You see, I told him, you needed some modicum of experience in order to 'survive', to be able to 'cope'. A sexual relationship was something you had to 'steel yourself for'.

'Where is the evidence for this? How come you're sure that sex is painful if you've never had sex?'

A piercingly good question, one that momentarily stopped me in my tracks. Eventually I replied, 'I don't know how I know. I just know.' Then I launched into another chaotic word tangle.

'Let's slow everything right down, take one step at a time with this.'

The room discreetly offered itself as a contemplative tabernacle. However, when J used an expression such as 'sexual intercourse', the space would immediately freeze over into a voiceless wasteland. My left hand would pat the base of my throat, and the right one would cross over it, hands flapping like a nervous dove. Slowing down was awful because it meant that hidden meaning might sneak out. And I was afraid, immensely afraid of what my own words might mean, even though I was supposedly inviting in that very thing.

Something had to be faced in sex, I kept telling him, although I was not sure what it was. That was why I needed a teacher. J remained calm, because even speaking about these matters frightened me. His poise conveyed that he took my experience seriously, that he was willing to try to help.

'If you could have worked out this problem on your own, with your logical faculty, you'd already have done so.'

He seemed to know how my weary intellect had battled with this conundrum. This was simply beyond its rational powers.

'You chose to enter into therapy. That was a most wise thing to do.' His affirming pragmatism was reassuring. 'You knew you needed help from another human being to extend your field of vision. Because you can't see the back of your head, can you? *I* can.'

(Sometimes, I would add, 'Yeah, then again, you can't see my face.')

Just once did J sweep through with what felt like an ultra-confident, male intervention. 'Of course, you know the facts about sex, don't you?'

Inside, I was desperate to cover up shame, to not expose my clumsy naivety to his penetrating searchlight. The call was to reassure him – yes, yes – to steer the conversation away from embarrassment, possibly for us both. The truth crept beneath the searing inner loneliness of *not sure.*

'The thing is,' I confided, forgetting that he did not need to be subjected to keeping-worries-at-bay strategies, 'I'm completely asexual.'

Long silence, rich with scepticism.

J replied, sounding certain of his facts. 'There is no such thing as being asexual.'

I was determined to cling to my life raft. 'Aren't you the lucky therapist, because you are working with the exception! I am telling you, I'm *totally* asexual!'

His Master's Voice rose again, sounding like Death tolling. 'You cannot *not* be sexual. You can only choose to be in relationship with your sexuality or not.'

A demoralised mood ensued as I pondered the implications of his statement. Did that mean I could never get rid of sexuality?

'For someone who's not interested in sexuality, you certainly like to talk about it, don't you?' J comments wryly. Deadpan humour eases our way into talking about the contradiction of how, on the one hand, I want to feel attractive to men but, on the other, I am afraid of what might be expected of me if I inadvertently evoke desire. And, of course, I have no desire myself.

'There was that one time at the disco ...'

Always J's explicit encouragement, 'Tell me about it. Just say whatever comes into your mind.'

His invitation is to relinquish my worried attempts to resolve everything today, to lay down this burden of heaviness, to let myself rest, even play in the space between us. It feels like an immense act of trust. I take up his cue and snuggle down on the couch.

'What age were you then?'

'Maybe sixteen ...'

J is sifting through the jigsaw of disjointed session pieces.

My first memories of settling in Northern Ireland at the age of six. Being in a playground, surrounded by children who seem impressed by me, and my English accent, particularly when I tell them that I've taken ballet lessons and could show them a few steps if they'd like. The children ask a funny question 'Are you a – ?' I've never heard their word before, so I don't know what it means. Everyone falls about laughing, not nastily, eyeing this exotic creature.

'How can you not know that?'

'Sure everyone knows that.'

The next day I'm able to give them their answer. 'No, I'm not a "Protestant",' because that had been the word. 'I'm a Catholic.'

Another memory. The first rented house when we moved to Northern Ireland, the one with the fabulous jungle of a garden.

We band of children spend long summer days play-ing in the rhododendrons and staying up late because my father, the disciplinarian, is away. The talk is of a dream house being built in another village, further removed from my newfound friends. When we move to this new town everyone calls me the 'master's daughter'. We are 'blow-ins'. We will be considered outsiders, even if we live here for the next century. I don't feel right about the gleaming tennis court that sets us further apart. We have a housekeeper. Somewhere I pick up talk that my parents have done something wrong. If they are going to create work, it should go 'to one of our own'.

The first bomb. No warning. I'm reading an adventure book in my bedroom. Then, for some reason, I put my book on the bedside table and go into the lounge. Suddenly, there's a big bang and the lights come crashing down. After the chaos, I find the book destroyed by glass and someone is saying, 'You'd have been cut to pieces.' The thought is odd: just like that you could be dead. Like the fish in the pond, killed by the explosion.

It goes from there, only it's mixed up. The shooting. The bombs. The house being destroyed. Moving away. Then Daddy wants us to go back. He's not going to give up. The dream house is to be rebuilt. I don't know if it's because of his beloved garden, or because there's nowhere else to go.

'... maybe I was seventeen at the disco.'

The teenage hours spent studying are a welcome retreat: the outside world can be made to not exist. However, my cousin has organised a school disco in Belfast and I am allowed to go. A boy with a nice face asks me to dance, first one bop, then another. I am trying out a brave new world of fun. Then the DJ shouts into his microphone, 'Last set.' The boy nods towards the door. 'Will we go outside?'

Suddenly I wonder how many session minutes are left because talking about this is useless. Words are futile, meaningless sticks tossed out to an imaginary dog.

J coaxes, 'Try to stay with this for a few minutes more.'

I am so exhausted, I can no longer form the words. 'This guy was looking at me ... and I felt ...' – how to describe it? – 'trapped.' Such a ridiculous expression. 'Going to be trapped ...' Every vestige of fun has drained away. Going through that disco hall door is a profound life-and-death decision. 'The boy will think I know what to do when I don't.'

The truth is that these confused feelings cannot be shared with anyone, because they live shut down in an air-locked pocket. J is drifting off behind an unreachable glass cage. '*Make* me understand. I want to come alongside.'

I can't, I can't. The space between us is a washed-out nothingness. All I can do is stack grey stones on that crumbling wall of language and connection. The sense of being real to myself, and to another, has died, which is how a part of myself feels inside.

J's voice lingers. 'You tell your story well. Curious, isn't it? How you tell it with so little emotion.'

Sometimes the man can be maddening.

'I don't know what you're talking about.'

Yet the same memories and images keep floating onto the couch, as though pressing for an outlet. A hinterland is increasingly opening up in sessions, where there is no delineation between imaging, sensing, remembering and speaking.

Fourteen years old. The night after St Stephen's Day. Car bomb left outside our front door. Aimed at the police station. There was a late warning, but I'd been sick in bed all day. We got trapped in the house, and the bomb went off. No home any more. Daddy's beautiful gardens, the summerhouse, the tennis court. All shattered.

My sister and I have to share a bedroom in a cramped rented house in another town. The days of having my own bedroom are over. My elder brother sleeps on the sofa.

My handsome daddy is gone. His body sits at the kitchen table, topped by an old face, as if someone has stolen the real him away. He's always busy these days, his desk covered in papers, obsessively talking about solicitors, claims, the Northern Ireland Office. He's forgotten about me.

Daddy's the one I lean on since we've been in Ireland; maybe it was Mummy earlier. When I have a nightmare, I sleep in Daddy's arms. I have a nightmare about getting trapped in a fire. Daddy says I'm not to worry, he'll show me in the morning how to climb out of the window. When daylight comes, he forgets. I think, 'It's silly, don't ask.' He is a charismatic god. He runs the family with a benign iron will.

Mummy is quiet. She might forget I've started my periods. That's why I'd fainted that morning. She hides the sanitary towels in the bathroom. Now we've a different bathroom. I'm not sure where to look for them anymore. I don't have any money to buy them if she forgets. The whole family are miserable. I'm the only unaffected one.

Sometimes the room is so still that when J speaks, it is a surprise. 'What if it was you who was upset?'

Me? *Me?* Someone has allowed for the unbeliev-able possibility that I am not always happy. There is the monumental impact of the same old story being recast with an entirely different meaning.

J proposes a series of hypotheses:

'What if the world looked depressed because you were seeing it through your own eyes?'

'What if you turned the situation the other way round in order to make it bearable?'

'What if you were depressed and the others were depressed as well?'

I am too shocked to reply.

The newspapers carry articles about therapy, controversial court cases and expert submissions. I am terrified that the bogeyman, a false memory, will leap out – aha! – making sense of the incomprehensible, but leaving my world, and the worlds of those around me, in ruins.

J emits good sense and normality. 'This is not necessarily about having been dropped on your head when you were six.'

A word seems to have emerged from nowhere, thrown up by the sea of the unconscious. I am saying, something, something, something ... 'exposed'.

J is attuned to the nuances, to the flecks of variation and colour that make up a human psyche. He is scanning the shore of language with intuition, skilfully feeling his way along the sand, sensing the texture of me. A pebble has caught his eye. There is the surrounding movement of heightened energy as he stretches down to pick it up. '*Exposed*,' he murmurs delicately, stroking the pebble in the palm of his hand. 'What does that make you think of?'

'Nothing.'

A light touch of encouragement. 'Go with the "nothing" thought.'

He has already told me it is hard to be thinking of nothing, and that is true.

Exposed.

Something is glistening on the horizon, a memory silted up out of the blue, his room superimposed with another room, my bedroom. I am twelve, maybe younger, maybe older. Those sequences are flickering in front of my eyes, that time I was nearly found out. No one must know.

'What are you thinking?'

It was the pact at the outset: speak out your thoughts and feelings. More and more times are accumulating when I cannot. Cannot talk about the bombs, about sexuality, about the family.

'I'm not thinking anything.'

He knows rightly, and I know rightly, that I am lying.

'You're withholding something.'

The room is tense as I try to figure out a plausible strategy to throw him off track.

'It is time.' His voice sounds flinty.

The walk from the couch to my coat to the door feels like the Grand Canyon.

It is over a late evening coffee in Bewley's coffee shop that the sick, worried feeling kicks in. A thought is forming: *Can't go on with therapy*. However, unbeknownst to me, one of those boomerangs that J talked about is whizzing across the night sky.

My world is about to be changed for ever.

2

Struck by lightning

A night full of talking that hurts,
My worst held-back secrets. Everything
Has to do with loving and not loving.
This night will pass.
Then we have work to do.

Rumi, 'A Man and a Woman Arguing',
translated by Coleman Barks

WHATEVER WAY I told him, J thought I had said, 'I've done a terrible thing.' (Now I wonder what I *did* say?) I kept repeating, 'A terrible thing has happened. It's Carmel.'

Carmel: my friend from home; my room-mate throughout college. Sweet-natured Carmel, who organised my twenty-first birthday party, who did the cooking and cleaning afterwards, and who, at midnight, arranged for the song 'Every Little Thing She Does Is Magic' to be played and everyone to dance around me.

I was distraught, struggling to convey what had happened and simultaneously wanting to obliterate the news.

'Carmel ... Been teaching in Portugal ... Coming home ... Not on the flight ... Alarm raised ... The school thought ... found ... wood ... days ... alone ... '

He was mirroring back the stark words in the newspaper report: raped, strangled. I was shouting at him, 'You're lying. It's a mistake. They've got the wrong person.' I was frantically burrowing into the threads of the couch, hoping that a cave would open up in which I could hide.

He called out my name. The far-off sound of my name sinking in.

J said, 'You know what has happened.'

And the terrible thing was that I did. I knew that Carmel had just been found, murdered by a stranger. Touch frightened me, but that day, oh God, that day, in madness, a cry rose up from the depths of inner devastation.

'Hold me.'

The words hung, unbearably aching. Silence. Silence. I knew no hug would take place; it was the therapeutic space itself that had to hold. Oh Jesus, the longing to be held in arms, the calling out for touch, so long shut out in terror, activated again by terror.

At the end of the session, I twisted my hands.

'Funeral ... can't ... what'll I do?'

The next week was Easter. There were no sessions during the Easter break. Outside, another patient was waiting, another life yearning to be cradled. J stood at his doorway and held out my woollen navy coat. For four months I had been enjoying my tart feminist gesture, informing him in a prim and proper voice, 'I can put on my own coat, thank you very much.' Now I was a child; doing up the buttons with trembling hands was too big a task. Carmel's murder was imprinted on the tangle of conscious and unconscious terrors I had brought along to my first session. Everything was about to crack open; there was nothing I could do to stop it.

He was helping me with my coat. I could feel my limp arms slip into one sleeve, then the other. He was placing the coat around my shoulders, letting his hand rest there for several moments. I could feel the imprint of a firm male hand, solid and reliable in a shapeless world. As if by osmosis, his calm inner strength seemed to flow into me, communing: Take courage. Take heart.

He was willing me on. No words. No hug. He was working within the strict confines of psychoanalysis, giving in the way he could. He was a very different person in those days. Then he was formal, reserved and almost shy.

Despite the notes I made at the time, it is impossible for this account to be verifiably accurate. I can only give an impression of how therapy was. It is like a flower. You cannot remember, well, was that the day the flower opened, or was it still in bud, or was it then that the petals fell and I believed that all life was wiped out?

'What will I do?' I whispered.

I do not remember exactly how he replied, yet always there was his refrain. 'I am here for you. The time is here for you. The room is here for you. Come back and we will find a way to be in this together.'

For one crazy moment I thought, *Could I sleep in his room at night, make soup on a gas stove, keep warm with a blanket? No one would find me. I wouldn't have to go to the funeral.*

Once I stepped out of the therapeutic room, Carmel's death would be undeniably true.

Someone else was waiting; someone else needed him.

We shook hands. That was our ritual when we had done good work, when we had faced fears, or even, God forbid, admitted that we enjoyed each other's company. The door closed behind me.

And my only thought was, *He will never hug me. Not ever.*

My parents are in the church for the removal ceremony. I do not know why but I cannot be with them. I have to weep broken-heartedly with my friends. I have decided to allow my grief out or I will go insane. The coffin is 'sealed', a numbing word. They say it is sealed for legal reasons, owing to the circumstances of Carmel's death. Is what has happened too horrific to show? No matter how she looks, I want to stroke her hair, kiss her goodbye and tell her we are all with her now.

The funeral is in two days' time. Friends are convening from all over Ireland and abroad. I remember, on the last day of college, I dived into an Oxfam shop and bought a collection of African mahogany baby elephants. Each friend got a present, a talisman to protect us and to sustain the link. We agreed that the elephants would have a reunion in ten years' time. It is six years on. The elephants are gathering for Carmel's funeral.

I am looking at my unrecognisable reflection in the mirror, talking to myself, 'Sometimes it's OK to cry.' I am following my friend Phil around like a child, begging her, 'Don't leave me.' She somehow understands that I am not just grieving for Carmel but for my life too. I am a tree split by lightning.

Phil lovingly fingers her father's memorial card:

Life is immortal.
Love is eternal.
Death is but a horizon
And a horizon is the limitation of our sight.

She recites that prayer, maybe fifty times, as we both look at the black church, crying. The time has come for the funeral. For a moment I get sick and think I am going to faint. Phil says, 'You don't have to go.' But I do.

We stand in the bitterly cold country church where one day we thought Carmel would be married and we would laugh and throw confetti. Phil is to my left; Gary, our college friend, is to my right. I need to know that there is such a thing as a good man who is appalled by violence. I need to hold that man's hand in mine.

Now we move outside to the darkening graveyard where I glimpse ghostly faces among the sorrowful snow-flakes and hear the bereft cries. It is senseless, but true: Carmel is dead. The final hour is coming, the rattling of earth. Is Carmel to lie in this remote grave, at the age of twenty-eight? And the world – what of the world with its horror? Will I climb in beside her, cover us both in clay so that she and I are not alone?

There is only the wind and the snow, the agony and the anger, the shattering of hearts. Perhaps, too, I can hear Phil's father as he stood with us that day: 'Life is immortal. Love is eternal.'

The room was cold, as it usually was first thing on Monday morning. There was the alcove with the impressive psychoanalytic books, the semicircle of chairs placed against the wall, the discreet box of tissues beside the couch. Usually we would go through our etiquette, two voices allowing the complexity of a life to reveal itself through the medium of a silent, alive space. But that day I think I curled up on the couch, as though it were a cot, and turned my head towards the solace of the wall. The portraits of Sigmund Freud, Carl Jung, and Roberto Assagioli, the lesser-known founder of psychosynthesis, stared down over the couch. The room was silent for a long while. Eventually J's voice softened the space.

'It seems hard to speak today.'

There was no known language that could communicate the experience of the previous week. 'Words are all we have,' J used to repeat, and often there was the call to the work, the unremitting discipline of therapy, the momentous struggle to give form to that which was unnameable, indescribable, which perhaps existed even before language, the gargantuan task of relating to another human being.

J encouraged, 'Try to speak.'

Weeping. Weeping. I could only utter one word: 'Carmel'.

Every attempt at communication was overthrown by sobbing, yet I could feel another presence forming: a mind reflecting, a body attending, a heart holding. He was listening closely to me, watching out for every broken breath, every racked sound. He was coming alongside my despair; he did not move from his chair.

J said, and he sounded biblical, 'Now it is the living who suffer and need our care.'

There was no point in clutching secrets or being afraid to speak what was already in my conscious mind. What did anything matter, when there was no God? On that day, in agony, words tumbled out, mixed-up associations about bombs, suffering, sex and fear. He was like a surgeon, deftly assessing the wounds, asking specific questions, sensing, quite rightly, that another time I might not have the courage to speak. He wanted to gather enough information to help. Shock had prised me open.

By 10.50 a.m. I was cried out. J said, 'I will see you on Wednesday.'

Two whole days away: how would I survive? Here was the hardest challenge – how to go back to my office when my heart was breaking and everything had been rent asunder. An hour later a colleague came over to my desk. 'Would you like a cup of tea?'

It was the small acts of kindness that made the process of living and therapy bearable.

There are sequences that I can tell J about. This is where his unflinching, sinewy capacity is helpful. It is important that he is not contaminated by my terror. I am frightened to go back to these memories but I am also frightened to be left alone with them at night.

Christmas 1975. The night after St Stephen's Day. Been sick in Mummy and Daddy's bed all day. Fainted in the morning, right out on the kitchen floor. One of my first periods. Still in my nightdress. Bleeding. How does this one begin? Telephone call? Shouts on the street? Daddy's running in. Car bomb outside. No time to get out. No lights on at the front of the house. Everyone thought we were away. Too dangerous to leave now. Last time when we were fleeing, the bomb went off in front of us. Going to hide in the corridor downstairs. The safest part of the house. Is that right? Feel I'm caught up in a black-and-white film, playing at the wrong speed. Daddy's frantic. Dark, long, narrow corridor. Four rooms off it: garage, elder brother's bedroom, my bedroom, sunroom. Daddy is dragging out mattresses. He's making an air-raid shelter, like something out of the Second World War.

I cannot go on. J had assured me at the end of the last session, 'I will go with you on this journey wherever you need to go, no matter how frightening it is. I will walk with you as long as it takes. We are in this together. I will not leave you.'

But the thing is ... the thing is ...

Everyone advised me, 'Put Carmel's murder out of your mind; remember the happy times.' But her death cast a deadly spell; it seemed compellingly unreal. J was my loyal rock. He offered the gift of being unafraid, faithfully applying his mantra balm: 'Everything can be included and spoken here. Nothing need be forbidden or censored. You can say anything at all. This is not like the outside world. This is not a conventional situation. Whatever you're thinking, say it, and we can hold it up to the light together.'

'Together' was the most comforting word in the English language.

I was afraid to go to bed. Night after night there were menacing nightmares: me hiding from faceless, hunting murderers; meeting myself in dreamland, crying, yet never able to discover what I was crying about; meeting a girl who had been attacked, terrified it was Carmel, terrified that it might be me. When I awoke, the bedroom would be black with panic. But when my tears had settled, and the dream had been confined to a scribble, I would soothe myself with the thought 'J says the psyche's trying to help me. He will be there for me tomorrow. I'm not on my own with this for ever. Just for tonight.'

J was taking care of me in a place of crisis, meticulously sifting through the flotsam of seemingly unconnected dreams, thoughts and memories, delivered in weekly bundles of sodden tissues.

'What does all this mean?' he would murmur, and propose his clarion call, 'Let's analyse this together.' But finding meaning was beyond me because I was lost in a sea of feelings. 'Wouldn't anyone be terrified?' I swivelled right round to look at him. 'Isn't the world a terrifying place?'

He was deep in his analytic reverie, leaning back in his armchair, his legs outstretched, his eyes closed, letting my inner world swirl over him while he kept us both anchored to his own secure harbour.

'You see ... Can't ...'

My ability to form coherent phrases was disintegrating. It was as if the string that holds the necklace of a sentence together had been wrenched off and the beads were scattering in a dozen directions. The words were like the fragmentation I felt inside. Leaving the session was a tremendous wrench.

'Could we end five minutes early so I've more time to gather myself before going back to work?' I asked.

'Try drinking a milky coffee after sessions,' J encouraged. He was suggesting that one traumatic experience could awaken the memory-sense of another from an earlier time, from even as early as baby and mother. It was another of his ingenious ideas, and it stayed with me. I began to allow myself the comfort of Bewley's milky coffee after sessions and felt slightly better.

I stopped going on management courses to learn how to put boundaries around work. I believed in J when he said that everything I needed to help me was in the room, if only I could learn how to access it. However, that meant I had to believe in the basic premise: that the external and internal worlds might be linked, that there *was* such a thing as an internal world. For me, that was one almighty step.

In the early weeks, work was often on my mind. One day, J mused, 'The senior-management structure is based in England, and you've no local support committee here?' I thought it was a good, pragmatic idea, one I had never considered, yet he was continuing, making interpretations, and what he was saying was completely off the wall, yet so brilliantly imaginative that it resonated inside, as if he was calling out to some wordless part of me, hiding.

'It's as if you're trying to expand yourself at work, to inflate in order to survive ... The sense is there are no parents ... There is no one there to help you ... You're all alone in the world, trying to mother yourself.'

In another session he added, 'You keep looking after other people's vulnerability rather than attending to your own. You offer the trainees on your media course this extreme nurturing and then you come in here and experience me as disappointingly harsh and severe.'

'That's not true.'

'You're projecting out your own internal fraughtness ...'

'Honestly!'

'... rather than taking it back to yourself and dealing with it. You are infantilising your trainees, whereas I treat you as an adult. Responsibility for the therapy rests with you.'

Christ.

And after the session – although J would emphasise, 'Let's think about this in the here and now' – I would reflect on his disturbing words: 'This constant busyness, these long working hours, this travelling to London and Dublin and God knows where else, is a defence against depression.'

It was not long before something interesting happened. Almost without noticing it, I started working on a radio programme in my spare time, with an encouraging producer. I had remembered what I enjoyed. J said I was moving back into contact with my deeper self.

In June 1989 I came in and announced that I had a new job: a one-year television-researcher contract. I could not figure out from J's frosty reaction what I had done wrong.

'You didn't discuss this with me beforehand.'

I was shocked that such a decision was supposed to be subject to analysis. I was used to doing everything on my own.

'I did this for us,' I said.

I knew that a fragile self was emerging, one that needed the couch to be free of the preoccupying clutter of work. I had also been thinking about a comment J had made one day, when I was feeling guilty about even contemplating leaving my job.

'You reproach yourself so much. This pattern of adversity and depression: it's like your father, isn't it? Not able to let go when wanting to get out of a difficult situation is understandable.'

I told J that I was worried about negotiating the time out of work for sessions.

'So, now you've put the therapy in jeopardy.'

What was the point of seeking his support when my good intentions were thrown back in my face, when he was an imperious emperor, lording over an analytic sky-kingdom, removed from the daily demands of this earth? Better to take the unjustified flak, to sort out the situation myself and to withdraw into the disappointment that could not know itself as anger.

In the room is an invisible Pandora's box, I tell J. It must not be opened or evil ghouls will be released.

'It?'

The inexplicable 'it'. At the same time, the theme of confrontation continues to ripple out from our first meeting. One day I ask J if the door is locked. I confess I almost want it to be locked, want him to force me to face up to memories. 'Confront me.'

'We can talk about these things,' he says, calmer than ever, his steady repetition creating an accumulative field of faith.

The power of psychoanalysis is unfolding. On the couch there is no distraction of a reactive human face, no intrusive response, no disapproval. A crazy thought is let float, and the not-understood flits around like a feather. J reintroduces the reality of the situation: the door is not locked. I test it myself once when I suddenly have to escape in the middle of a session. So easy to be on the other side of the door where people shuffle up and down the stairs.

'You are free to go at any stage. It is you who chooses to speak.'

I think to myself: *he is giving me back my power.* J reminds me: hope is also in Pandora's Box.

Two tidal energies are pulling me apart: the part that yearns to release words, so that they are not eternally churning inside, and the part that cannot bear to face the reality of those words. A force presses down – Speak! – but there is a pain in my throat, as if a sliver of shattered glass has become lodged there. There goes that word again.

I had rung J in despair. 'There's no point in us going on. I'm wasting your time and mine. I'm never going to be able to speak. I'm really sorry.'

Sometimes, when I catch him off guard, he sounds warmer than the depriving severity of his pared silences. J says, 'We can talk about this on Wednesday. We can try another approach.'

I am surprised – is there another approach?

His voice emits confidence. 'Just turn up.'

Here I am again. Courage is about to break through, nursed by his hypnotic lullaby: 'I have heard many, many things as a therapist. Nothing you say can shock me.'

He had proved his unswerving trustworthiness in the aftermath of Carmel's death.

It is an Indian summer morning in September 1989. I have promised myself that today is the day or I am handing in four sessions' notice. I need to speak, don't I? Yes. This is it.

I do as I always do on Monday mornings: I get there early, wangling my way into the building. I wait outside J's door and sense him arriving through sounds. First, the footsteps echoing up the staircase – determined, resolute, male – someone emphatically his own person, not afraid to be himself. Then the formalised cadences, tinged with optimism. 'Good morning. Come in. It will warm up soon.'

Outside, diggers are pounding, workmen shouting, drills rattling. The street below is being dug up for cable lines. It is almost funny: the day I have chosen to speak is the one day I will have to battle to be heard above the din.

'I'm sorry about this noise. We'll do our best, as we always do.'

I lie down on the couch, hiding my head under my protective arms. Say the words. Start, because if you haven't said them by ten to eleven, you're leaving therapy. Silence. Silence. God, the anxiety-inducing pressure of silence. Steel body, close eyes. Do it. The first word: 'breasts' (cringing); spit out, 'nipples' (ashamed, afraid). OK, try another: begins with an s, 's-h-a-r-p.' Put them in twos: 'sharp things'. The one with an r, 'ritual'; the hard one, 'vagina'; now a small one, 'pain'. You can do it, you can say it all or you'll never have the guts to again.

There are words that day that are for him and for me. I am telling J about the rituals I had for a long time in late childhood and teenage days, my attempts to ready myself for the pain I associated with sexuality. This is what 'exposed' had meant to me. For fifty minutes I relentlessly will myself to speak, and he is with me all the way, ever clinical but he wants to help. I know he does.

At last my catalogue of misery has been spewed out. I have never heard these words spoken aloud to another human being, or even heard them myself. The rituals that frightened and fascinated me simply took me over and had to be done.

'I want to say something to you before we end,' J says.

It is rare for him to initiate an intervention like this. My head recedes into the couch, quaking with dread. He articulates my name with great sincerity.

'I want to acknowledge how much courage you've had here today. You've shown *so* much courage.'

He could have made a thousand brilliant interpretations, yet at this pivotal moment, my lowest hour, he chooses to respond from the heart with compassion. A beautiful quality, like angel dust or healing sunlight, is falling into the room and, with it, the sense that the two of us are being held in the deepest connection – that of spirit. He is meeting me and caring for me in all of who I am. He has not rejected me, my secret terror.

The moment feels transcendent, yet also of this earth. There seems to be some paradoxical connection between the naming of the dark and the emergence of light, between going to the terrifying edge – risking trust in another – and, in that integrity, being honoured by the universe. There had also been something important about speaking rather than writing, because J had kept reiterating: 'That which cannot be spoken will be acted out.'

He knows a little more about me now. I have to hope that things will be OK between us.

'We can think about this together. We have all the time in the world we need.'

Time is billowing out like a safe, cloudless sky.

'We can come back to this again. You've made such a good beginning.'

He seems still, not horrified, as if he is remembering with rapt concentration not simply every word I have uttered but the exact sequence of how I have linked them. There is no over-the-top sympathy, no patronising denial of what I have shared, no scurrying for hot tea in a flurry. He is letting me have my dignity, after I have revealed my most wretched scars. It is his respect for me – his love – in these fifty minutes that move me beyond words.

I did not look at J as I self-consciously scuttled out, but, stepping into the street, I felt an exhilarating relief. A trapped knot of fear and hurt, consuming copious amounts of energy in having to be kept hidden, had become slightly untangled. The words were out in the world now, and the tiniest possibility for freedom had opened up. It had been a terrible day, a sacred day, and there was no contradiction in these two concepts resting side by side. I was dancing on air, past workmen, past the postman, past the women whose curls from the humble hairdresser looked lovely to me.

Later, I thought, *'Beginning'? Sure, what more is there to say?* Elation had ebbed away, and terror had me locked again in its vicious stranglehold. I did not know that traumatic experiences have to be worked, and reworked, over long periods before they settle inside, like sand after a big storm.

When J and I next met, it was as if the previous session had never happened. Later he would steer me back to the agonising material; for now he was wise and did not. He trusted in me and in the nature of the psyche. He was willing to wait patiently until I was ready to speak again. I could feel my taut self creep out into the strong holding presence of the room/couch/him. I could let myself recover from my own words and experience the hope of being allowed to just be.

Yes, definitely, we would go on.

One day I wondered aloud whether if I stole out into life and forged a sexual relationship, the same fate would befall me as Carmel? Was her death a warning? I had the freedom to air my unhealthy terrors. J had already gone over the statistical likelihood of another murder occurring. That had not helped. His body was shifting; he was going to claim the territory between us with conviction.

'This is not how it can be between two adults, between a man and a woman, when there is choice and agreement. What happened to Carmel is different.'

I was listening intently. He was a therapist, and he was a man, and he was standing up for consensual pleasure, for love. I was shocked at myself. Did I really believe

that sexual relationships were based on coercion and violence? Somewhere, in the gripping unconscious, I did. I
was ashamed of my crippling innocence, but I had to ask:
'J, are you absolutely sure?'

Three golden arrows rang out with astounding
impact.

'I am sure.'

In the way he said those words, I suddenly knew
that he loved someone very deeply. Those were the most
important words that anyone said to me at a most terrible
time in my life.

In October 1989 I decided to move out of my aunt's house
– in order to give her new relationship some space – but,
within a month, I was struck down with a chronic form
of arthritis. For one week I was unable to get along to J
because of being in hospital. It was frightening how my
world was breaking down.

Now, weak and recovering, I lie on the couch, desperate to understand what is happening to me. I find myself
telling J about the days immediately after the terrible
bomb in 1975. J asks, 'Why has this come into your mind
at this juncture?'

A good question, but I do not know the answer.

*Mummy and Daddy have sent my brothers and sister away
to relatives but I won't leave them in their hour of need. So I'm
the only one allowed to sit in the rubble of a kitchen. I'm not to go
into other rooms because the structure of the house is shaky. Poor
Daddy is upset. He wants me to help him board up the windows.
It's hard to hold the torch steady in the night wind and rain. At last
a neighbour turns up. Daddy says he couldn't have done it without*

me, that I was his excellent helper. You see, I was special. He needed me. I didn't let him down.

J's room has become penetratingly cold. I need to get warm with my coat, which is hanging over by the door. The space between it and me is too large to manage, after my recent illness. I ask J, 'The room's got cold. Could you please get me my coat? I'm so stiff. I don't think I can get it.'

Silence. From far off, J replies: 'The room is actually very warm.'

He does not understand. The unforgiving blackness, the shards of glass, the vulnerability are all on the couch, not as a recollection in memory but as pitiless reality. The past *is* the present. And I've gone terribly cold.

'J, I'm really cold. Could you get me my coat, please?'
Silence.

'The room is quite warm.'

And there is the frustration and the grief that I cannot make myself understood, and he who could easily give me what I need – something physically protective and comforting – is going down an intellectualising track. There is only one thing for it. I will have to huddle up and survive on my own. At last, the dreadful session comes to an end. I limp over to my coat, feeling sick, upset and alone, existentially alone in the world.

'I will see you on Wednesday.'

J's voice sounds normal; he does not realise how it has been for me. However, there will be no second session that week, because by Wednesday I will have been admitted to a second hospital.

For months I had been thinking about how I would like to talk to my mother, to understand our family story. Then I fell ill. My mother was by my side in the second hospital and looked after me later while I recuperated at my parents' house. 'Your father and I saw your vulnerability at Carmel's funeral. We want to help. You were such a happy child.' I hear her longing for that child to return. A warm relationship is glimmering, quite different to the cold mother figure who has dominated my internal world.

The family never speaks about the past, so I have to give my mother no hint about my therapy. She tells me something I did not know: 'We were offered family counselling. I turned it down. I thought we had suffered enough.'

J's question comes back into my mind: 'Why did nobody intervene?'

She adds, 'Don't you remember? You didn't speak for days after that bomb. We were so worried about you. We thought we'd have to take you to a psychologist. All you did was follow your Daddy around. You were a pathetic wee figure, clinging to your father.'

It was the end of my first year in therapy. I had imagined my life would be glowing with wisdom, transformed by a fairytale wave of a wand.

My life was in tatters.

In the last session before Christmas 1989, J murmured, 'You've had a savage first year.' I thought to myself, to my friend the couch, that's a good adjective to describe it. I found myself telling J about a poem that was often in my mind these days, Raymond Carver's 'Late Fragment.'

And did you get what
you wanted from this life, even so?
I did.
And what did you want?
To call myself beloved, to feel myself
beloved on the earth.

I told him that I had once read an article by Carver's
wife, Tess Gallagher, who noted that part of the poem's
beauty was that it was written by a recovering alcoholic
who had struggled for a long time yet had finally come to
this miraculous point, where he could accept and know
himself as loved.

Then I started to cry and could not stop.

'I keep thinking about Carmel, how she'll never have
a chance for love and' – sobbing – 'I can't feel beloved
myself.'

Life was inexorably raw. Most likely I would lose my
contract as a researcher because of my illness. Therapy
would be over anyway because I would no longer be able
to afford it. It would all have been in vain.

J's voice was full of comfort. He was holding on to
hope for me, the hope I could not hold onto for myself.
'Hope is always there. Look where the journey has taken
you – such a long way from the beginning – and who
knows what next year may bring? Perhaps with time, and
work, and talking, all things might be possible.'

3

The human circle

Group analysis is not so much concerned with the question of how people have become what they are than with the question: what changes them or prevents them from changing?

S.H. Foulkes, *Therapeutic Group Analysis* (c. 1964)

IT WAS clear that therapy was going to take longer than I had originally thought and that I needed more support, given the extent of what was unravelling inside me. But I could not afford more sessions. It was then that J suggested combined therapy, explaining that, although unusual in Ireland, the approach was well established in the United States.

Apparently it was possible to undertake therapy, both individually and in a group, where every member of that group shared the same therapist. Confidentiality was crucial, so there was no contact between members outside the weekly group. There was also an additional fee, although J offered me a reduced, all-in rate.

'The group includes both men and women and has been going for a while. People join and leave. The experience can be the equivalent of a full-blown analysis.'

Aren't I already in that? I thought.

Combined therapy sounded like an intriguing secret society. Did I imagine my relationship with J being affected? Probably not, or I would not have put that at risk. My mind cannily split the 'group' and 'individual' into two distinct categories, and, if the whole experience did not work out, I assumed that I would just revert to individual therapy and make do.

The hairdresser's shop looks glum in the early evening light of March 1990. Some people are at the doorway so I do not need to buzz up to gain entry. When I knock on J's door, this time there is only a shout back: 'Come in.'

He has not personally come out to greet me, has not solicitously offered to take my coat, not glided to his armchair in perfect synchronicity with my movements to the couch. Our precious *pas de deux* is falling away, now that we are more than two.

On entering, I see that J is working at his desk in the far corner of the room and that the usually empty alcove facing me now has a circle of nine chairs. I sit alone in the circle, listening to J shuffling papers, and let a changed world order sorrowfully settle.

Buzz.

A man in his late thirties comes in. I hold out my hand as if at a party.

'Hello.'

Is this what I am supposed to do? God knows. Soon there are six people in the circle – three women, including me, three men, including J, and three chairs lying empty. J gives a nod to each person, and an awkward silence descends. It is their group, their world. I wish J would help.

They seem to be waiting for someone whom they stoically accept will turn up late. In he blusters, a big man, broad smile, noisily zipping and unzipping bags.

The woman with the kindly older face turns to me: 'I'm Anna. You're welcome.'

You are for ever bonded to the one who invites you into the group. She ushers in the opening sequence by introducing herself. I am relieved: I can take time to listen.

Through the window of first impressions, I see this group's dynamics in a way that later fades through familiarity. My initial reaction is that I like each person individually, although, en masse, they seem very different to me. Four, including both women, are in their forties or fifties, another generation. One man, Damien, remembers me from the psychosynthesis weekend, although, shamefacedly, I do not remember him (that is how I am with men). Another man, Tom, I have often seen on the staircase yet never ventured a hello, being intimidated by his stern demeanour.

What strikes me most is the lack of camaraderie between the two women, although each extends friendliness to me. As both speak of their chosen celibacy, I feel disappointed that there is no woman here trying for a sexual relationship with a man, no teacher to help me. The men dominate with their cut-and-thrust assertions.

Each person reveals what has brought him or her into therapy, as an introduction for me. The members cover the gamut of society, except for three important omissions: no one is in their twenties, except me, and no one is married or has children, except J. (From my chair I can see the photograph of three little ones clambering over sea-rocks, who must be the daughters to whom he occasionally refers.)

Is being single a sign of psychological ill-health? I wonder dispiritedly, as yet another person reveals 'I'm single.' Does it mean that something is not right, even though, intellectually, I disagree with this notion? Does J go home to a beautiful wife and gorgeous children and a roaring fire and thank God that he is not like the rest of us, doomed to combined therapy?

Everyone is seeing J individually once a week, so this is my first dilemma: should I keep my twice-weekly involvement secret for fear of provoking jealousy? I don't know. I feel young and shy with them.

J says nothing. Only one member's introduction left then. Maybe I want to be a *good* group member, whatever that means, for J's sake, to be self-revealing and not let him down. I want everyone to tell him afterwards, 'That's a fantastic woman.' Then J will be obliged to rethink the psychological failings he increasingly identifies in me.

Even I am surprised when I disclose that I have entered therapy because of difficulties with sexuality. The words hover, vague and nebulous, and later I will regret this degree of self-exposure.

Yet, now, a sense of group history is emerging. They tell me that they started out as a group two years before, and that, since then, two members have left. One leave-taking had been exceptionally challenging. An uneasy thought is growing: has J brought me in because of *his* needs, because his group was stuck and he needed a bright new catalyst? The speculation is that the two absent members – a man and a woman apparently – have stayed away because of ambivalence about my joining. Apparently I am the first newcomer since the group's original formation. I glance across at J, bewildered at this information, which contradicts what he had previously told me. I immediately want to offer to withdraw.

There follows a conversation amongst them all that I do not understand. J is questioning the members' version of group history and wondering what might be happening for people that this version is being presented to the newcomer.

I plough on and ask the members how does combined therapy work for them? Do they save up incidents for one setting or another, and how do they know what to bring where? They begin exchanging experiences, and I listen, a fascinated observer. The room hums with the cadences of the first people I have ever met who know what a psychoanalytic-based therapy is like, who confirm that J and the couch are not figments of my imagination. I find myself thinking, *God, they're depressed. Not like me.*

In the final fifteen minutes of the hour-and-a-half group session, J speaks. He proffers an elegant summation of the evening's underlying themes, tying what people have shared in a neat psychoanalytic bow that seems both highly intelligent and a touch loftily removed. Apparently, he had been at some cohesive gathering.

I wish I had been at his one.

In my second evening in the group, I told the members about Carmel's death. Damien said, 'I almost envy you. It's like you've been split open and can feel in a way I can't.'

After the Easter holidays, I came in and covered the couch with a jumble of words, sliding into a long protracted silence. Eventually J murmured, 'I am wondering that you haven't mentioned Carmel's first anniversary mass.'

That was the day I learned that psychoanalytic theory was true. You can split off and deny things that are too disturbing to take in. You lock them in some secret internal vault, hoping they will never return. But they sneak back in, swaddled in a disguise called a symptom.

The night graveside prayers are more heart-breaking than the funeral, if that's possible. Some of us are asked back for tea to Carmel's family house and invited to see her bedroom. I'm staring at pristine clothes, childhood books and toys, awaiting her return. Then I see him, standing guard over her bed: the baby elephant I gave Carmel. Excoriating rage rises up. How could I have been stupid enough to think that an elephant from Oxfam could keep anyone safe in the face of violence? The baby elephant bows his head: he may be one inch high, yet his features emanate gracious dignity. The elephant is still there, even though Carmel is gone and will never be coming back.

At times the couch mood could be like beautiful sad music, punctuated with J's soulful questions.

'Can you find a way to stop torturing yourself with Carmel's death?'

'Can you cultivate a new relationship with suffering?'

'Can you show yourself compassion?'

I would think, *No. Afraid of what uncontrollable deluge might be released if I do.* But another wave of tears would take over, and an inner voice would whisper, *Enter his compassion, even if you can't find any for yourself.*

Small words had a profound impact in his room. J watched over me with care, and with his art. Once, he said, 'If you can't breathe, I'll breathe for you.'

We were one and the same: mother and child. We would get through this together.

I had been searching for a patient's account, someone who could share what a modern-day therapy was really like. I could not find one. J had mentioned that he was interested in research. I enjoyed writing, so I decided to document my experience in a series of letters to him.

> *Letter extract, 10 March 1990*
> I want you to keep these letters for me until I finish therapy, no matter when that will be. I hope they will record the shifts, changes, crises and developments within the process. I would love to read them at the end, see the whole picture and write up my experience.

J could be a demanding taskmaster, like one of those wizened monks who teach meditation by propping apprentices over a well, with the dire instruction, 'Stay awake'. You would not survive if you did not toughen up.

His needling comments, particularly in the group, could feel hurtful. If you got nicked, too bad. Sometimes it came across as if he had forgotten that you were a human being and got carried away with his own glittering interventions. Over time, he changed, became less afraid to include his heart – or maybe that was me.

A few weeks after joining the group, I was struck down with another debilitating attack of arthritis. The doctor removed the fluid from my swollen left knee and bandaged my entire leg, insisting that if I did not rest in bed, worse damage could follow. However, it was Monday, and Monday meant both an individual and a group session.

That evening, I winched myself out of bed and took a taxi to the city centre. Limping into J's room, I lowered myself into the first available chair, manoeuvring a second one to prop up my gammy leg. Then I realised that I was sitting in the chair J usually occupied. He looked quizzically at me when he came over to join the circle. I was too tired to move.

The group was going fine until one of the men mentioned that he found me attractive. I immediately felt embarrassed that such a thing could be thought, never mind spoken. It had never occurred to me that sexual attraction might be a legitimate subject for group conversation. I hoped that J would growlingly intervene, but J did not seem to have the remotest intention of telling the man to stop.

Anna responded, 'Isn't that a lovely thing to say?'

I felt worse. That is how I should have reacted, instead of staring at the floor, frozen.

J stirred. 'Isn't her bandage fetching?'

I felt mortified. Was J mockingly accusing me of using my illness as a means of manipulating attention? Was resting a bandaged leg on a chair, as medically advised, really a woman giving a sexual come-on to a man? I was openly furious with J. How could he spout such a sexist thing? J was pontificating on the semantics of his language, elaborating that 'to fetch' meant to bring someone something. He noted that I was sitting in his chair, keeping my leg out of the group, obliquely cutting myself off. Illness certainly got me gains, generated visibility. His words felt invasively unfair and cruel.

There was nothing I could do other than withdraw into silence. The dreadful evening went on. Two people were arguing, their voices accelerating into a row.

At the end of the session, J wondered about the sequence. Could there be any connection between the two people expressing anger and my illness? Could they be acting out what my body was unconsciously communicating? And what was the underlying conflict that could not be expressed?

That evening was the first of many when I went home upset, wishing I had never heard of the group or of therapy.

My health continued to deteriorate. Determined to stave off a third stint in hospital, I booked an extra individual session with J. When I had settled down on the couch, J surprised me by seizing the initiative and speaking first.

'I rarely say anything. If I do, it is because I've got something important to say. You know I would terminate the therapy if I didn't think it was advantageous to you. Therapy is not for mad people; they couldn't handle the discipline of it.'

This was my repeated accusation: that therapy could precipitate insanity.

'No. Therapy creates an opportunity to not immediately react to circumstances but take the time to think what's *really* going on here.'

He talked about the past few grim weeks. 'You experience my words as a criticism of your lifestyle.'

I invariably felt met with silent disapproval when I talked to J about my involvement in the media. I always thought of the other women in the group, all in the traditional female professions, the ones of which I sensed J approved – caregivers, like my parents, and like both maternal and paternal grandparents and great-grandparents. I was the one who had promised my father that I would uphold the family tradition by becoming a teacher.

'I hold up a mirror to you,' J said. 'You don't like what you see, so you want to smash it. If it didn't press a nerve, it wouldn't hurt.' He went on, 'You experience yourself as loving to me and that I don't respond. In the middle of this distress, the confrontational is a central motif to you. Everything has to be organised into these rigid concepts of black and white, right or wrong. You defend the physical meaning of your illness and you polarise me as the adversary flying the psychological flag. Or you're in conflict with this immobilising illness and it becomes the enemy, or I'm the enemy, or the group is. You keep saying you're defeated, which means that someone or something is victorious.

'Look, if this illness was entirely organic, I could only support you as best I could, but we can also look at other psychological possibilities. After all, that's what you pay me to do, to make interpretations. It is such a masculine illness, isn't it, authoritarian and restrictive? It won't allow you out to play. A strict-father sort of illness.'

The bold creativity of his interpretations strikes.

'What about your inner conflict with Father, the tug between the idolised and hurtful aspects of him?'

(*No. Not going there.*)

'And your attraction to me?'

(I have confessed on the couch that there is no other man in the group to whom I am attracted.)

'Can you talk about that?'

(*I don't know that I can.*)

'There's your conflict between wanting to be an autonomous, independent adult, free to have sexual relationships, and being a child yearning to be picked up and cared for.'

I hear that he is telling me to pull myself together. I rally: 'I'll stop being self-indulgent then. I'll be sunny.'

His next comment unexpectedly touches my heart.

'No. It's like a child climbing up onto her mother's knee. You wouldn't do it unless you needed to.'

In that moment, I feel exquisitely understood in my vulnerability. I can hear him.

'Aren't there more healthy ways of getting affection, of having your needs met, by moving into adult relationships rather than reverting to being a child?'

I have never thought of adult relationships like that. That is a new framing of possibilities.

'There is no doubt that there's something genuinely wounded within you. You project that out. You locate that inner confrontation on to me.' He veers into a passionate declaration: 'Work this out in therapy, not outside.

Save yourself from trouble and heartbreak. Therapy is like a poultice, drawing out the hurt in order to heal. The dark belongs *in here*. Bring what belongs to therapy into therapy. We can work with it, explore it and perhaps transform it, so the outer world has the possibility of change. You don't have to blindly act it out.'

Suddenly I hear that he wants good things for me, that he believes in me. I feel my resolve strengthening.

'I want to try again.'

As I put on my coat, his words rinse through my being: 'Therapy is the process of working through problems that have been going on for years and choosing to face them. It is working from a bad self towards a strong inner self.'

A few days later my illness lifted, although intellectually I could not explain why.

In the following group session, I felt publicly belittled again when J referred to my additional session as an extra 'feed', linking it to another of his favourite psychological themes: the Good and the Bad Breast. But three months later, my doctor confirmed the return of health and I was able to write to J:

Letter extract, 1 July 1990
I can see that my illness did have a psychological meaning. I was trying to communicate something – a loneliness, loss and fear – that couldn't be put into words.

The individual cosseted cocoon was over. It was obvious: the group was the wife J truly loved, not me.

Jangled feelings were raked up, of wanting to keep him exclusively to myself, and knowing that this was impossible, yet still yearning. Every week I made sure to get to the group early, in order to sit immediately next to J, to hide under his feathers. Yet I resented being exposed – that bloody word again – in front of everyone as a pathetic child. I hated the needy little one in me.

One morning a dream captured my struggle with combined therapy. I was in a circle that I knew to be the group, yet everyone in it was a child. The other children were older than me and studying difficult school exercises. I was talking to them about the preoccupying themes of my life – my recurring arthritis, my longing to be free – but their heads did not lift. J came over to me. He whispered that I did not have to sort everything out straight away; I could take one thing at a time. He gave me a book with a colourful cover and inside it were poems and stories for a very young child. While everyone else was working, he pulled up his chair and stayed with me as we read my book together.

I had only been in the group for three months when I first walked out. One of the men mentioned that he could strangle his girlfriend – a meaningless, nothing remark. Inside I thought, *Murder's in here too.* Then a woman, building on the zigzag of free association, talked about the recent death of a friend and how good it had been to have time for goodbyes. Suddenly I felt a sick panic. Even though someone was in the middle of speaking, I got up and left the room.

Five minutes before the group ended, I returned and apologised.

J said, 'Don't apologise. Analyse.'

Early the following morning I was still upset. At 3 a.m. I switched on the light and wrote to J about another recent nightmare. In this one I had been in a car with a colleague, Philip, travelling along a lonely, ominous road in the pitch black of night when we drove over a pair of shoes. We stopped to get out, and I recognised that the shoes were Carmel's. In that horrendous moment I knew that somewhere, out there in the black wood, Carmel was lying dead. However, I begged Philip not to search for her because that would mean leaving me. We drove on to an empty house. Philip went upstairs to ring the police. Then, when I was downstairs, feeling alone and anxious, a man and a woman walked in. And I knew: these two had killed Carmel and now they were coming to kill me.

In the following couch session, J said, 'Let your mind drift. What are your thoughts and associations with the man and woman? Who do they remind you of?'

I was worn out fending off nightmares. I had to let the words take me where they wanted to go, to talk about the mother/father figures stalking my internal world, and the persecuting guilt that I might be betraying the family by speaking ... or by being angry.

I have come to Eckhart House, the Irish Institute of Psychosynthesis and Transpersonal Theory in Dublin, for a weekend course, drawn by the haunting title, 'Woman in Search of Herself.' Memories are shifting in response to a series of self-reflective questions.

The excitement of being alone with Daddy on a forest walk, him showing me a flower's features, telling me a secret: stamen, pollen, man, woman, something about the facts of life, how I need to be careful. I'm afraid of ruining everything by confessing, 'I don't understand.' All I want is for this closeness, this pervading security, to go on for ever.

Another day. Daddy is telling me about periods. I've been worrying about these scary towel things advertised in my Jackie *magazine. He gives me a book to explain it. Goes away, then comes back again, as if he's forgotten to mention something. 'Of course you can talk to your mother when it happens.' No. Daddy is the hero. Daddy is the key-holder to sexuality, because my period arrived a week later. Without him, I would have known nothing.*

The disgusting, loathsome touch of a sanitary towel. Leaving the towel's peel-back sticky paper behind in the bathroom by mistake. Should have kept it hidden. Overhearing Mummy sigh, 'I don't know how you're going to survive.' Inside I heard a prophecy of doom.

Now a horrible image is configuring in my internal landscape, in response to a guided meditation. I immediately want to destroy it – except the external woman's voice is suggesting otherwise.

'Can you trust the first image that is emerging? Try not to censor it. Be receptive.'

Coming into visualised form is a grotesque, crust-infested clam, shell clinging tightly to tense shell.

'What is the quality of the image?'

The overriding quality is of fear-stricken defensiveness. This clam is as old as time immemorial. I hate its every despicable feature.

'Let your image grow.'

Crouching in the image's recesses, I can make out the irrational panic, which is only intensified by having to hide. Beyond that lies a reservoir of loving goodness, seemingly inaccessible.

'If you are willing, talk with the image.'

I stare resentfully at the thing. An idea comes in: I could summon up a sledgehammer – bloody well force that object to open up, but I am afraid of killing the outer shell. I don't know how else to fix the problem that I don't understand.

'Can you ask what the image needs? Be open to the response.'

I am surprised when a female voice speaks: the clam is not an 'it'. Her wart ugliness lessens as she delivers a compassionate message: 'I want you to appreciate the enormity of the task you are undertaking, the huge fear inside, the wall of defences, and how very, very difficult it is to open up. Can you acknowledge me as your protector, that I kept you and your sexuality safe for a good reason?'

The clam espies the hammer and her voice rings out clear. 'I do not need brutality.' My heart feels for her. The hammer recedes.

'Has your image a name?' asks the guiding woman.

Her name is 'the Frightened Clam', for I know that this clam is bound up with my own shamed sense of virginity, with the pure terror of sexual intercourse (such a forbidden act of intimacy and trust), with the anguished feelings that I long to release in therapy, yet, agonisingly, cannot express.

As I rest into the meditation, a new thought is inspired about this clam which I know to be a part of me. The clam-me could be prised apart by an outside agent, or she could open up at her own pace. The clam confides that she thinks the latter is the way forward.

'It is time to say goodbye. Perhaps the image has something to say or a gift to help you.'

The clam looks at me lovingly. 'Appreciate the Frightened Clam,' she mouths before disappearing.

It was months of painstaking work before J and I got to this point on the couch.

The night after St Stephen's Day. Crouching in the corridor. Body stiff. Waiting. Waiting for the bomb to go off. Thud. Thump. Someone is moving upstairs. A gunman. A gunman is taking over. Burglars steal during bomb scares. If the bomb doesn't kill us, the gunman will shoot us. Whatever happens, we're going to be murdered tonight. I know I'm imagining these sounds. The waiting silence is making me insane.

Then Daddy's shouting up the stairs, 'Who's there?' A wave of shock. The sounds upstairs are real. Daddy hears them too. Then another, body-petrifying, no-breath notion: Daddy's afraid, *and the pitiless thought,* Daddy doesn't know what to ... *And then ... and then ... the look on Daddy's face. Mustn't breathe or the gunman will hear me. Must get ready for death. I'm bleeding, bleeding. Death is circling inside and outside me. I am alone, crossing over into some other world.*

I need J to be as he is, placing his experience, skills and knowledge at my disposal. In my mind's eye, J's iron grasp is holding on to me as the feelings crash in and down. He is murmuring so that only I can hear, something about the girl who must have been so very frightened.

I call out, 'Stroke my hair.'

The earliest memory-sense of comfort has come in, of fingers stroking my wispy fair hair. J will not remove my pain as an act of respect. The therapy is to be allowed to follow its own course, for I am back in the entombed corridor, only this time I am not alone.

I'm screaming and screaming, yet nothing seems to be coming out of my throat. No one can hear me scream, a horrific experience, as if I've been reduced to an inhuman void. The car bomb is exploding, swallowing up my feeble sounds in its giant's roar. There is black. There is blue. The house is rocking, the bedroom door flying off with the force of the explosion. Windows are disintegrating inwards with a mesmeric beauty, showers of glass dancing in chunks. The bedroom is lit up in a halo of light and smoke. The roof is collapsing on top of us. Glass in the sunroom is shattering. Shatter, shatter, shatter.

The noise has stopped. Lethal glass is everywhere. A dull nothingness descends as if death has arrived only I'm not fully dead. Or maybe I am, I just don't know it yet. Someone is crying. My mother has Valium to hand. No one seems dead or seriously injured. I think we are alive. I feel no pleasure or relief. The British Army has arrived. A soldier is shouting down the stairs with a clipped English accent, beaming torchlight onto the rubble. He looks about seventeen. He has been throwing up, his face green-white. He says, 'Sorry.' My mother says, 'I wish I could offer you a cup of tea.'

Only one thought is pummelling through my body-brain: No one must ever touch me. *If no one takes me in their arms or holds me close, I will survive. I can keep this mad-making sensation sealed tight within the parameters of body. Nothing will terrifyingly seep out.*

Standing in my nightdress, in the freezing December garden. The emergency floodlights from the police station eerily blink on, like in a science-fiction film. Men in uniforms swarm around. I turn and look at the house that was our home until a few minutes ago. The roof has caved in, leaving a sunken crater and ripped patchwork gaps. Every window is smashed, slates buckled. Home has collapsed. I don't know where we'll sleep tonight. I'm bleeding and bleeding. The blood won't stop. I don't know where to find the sanitary towels. The bathroom has been destroyed.

Perhaps J was killed as I led him down to the couch-corridor of impending death.

'The session is ending in a few minutes. I want you to sit up. That's right. Place both feet firmly on the floor. Good.'

The body that was once mine has floated out of its frame and is drifting far, far away into some grey tundra. The body has gone into exile and can never come back to me.

J asks, 'Is there anything you want to say to me before you leave?'

Mute shake of my head.

'Is there anything you need from me?'

A comforting question that makes me feel safe and cared for, as if he would grant my request if he could. Mute shake of head.

In the café afterwards, I drink a bitter-tasting coffee. I cannot go straight back to work. For the first time in fifteen years, the words have found me out. A crack has appeared in the glacier, which is enough for now.

The extent of my denial shocks me, the years I have spent convincing myself that feelings can be obliterated if they are deprived of oxygen, and knowing that this never has been, and never will be, true.

'Why didn't you get out when there was a warning?'

Perhaps J and I are unconsciously playing out a court case on the couch, the details of which I will not know until the therapy is over.

So J is the judge, and I am my father, defending himself in a small rural community against the Northern Ireland Office's devastating accusation of 'negligence'.

The British government is contesting our claim for compensation. In the courtroom is a policeman being asked whether or not, in the panic of the night, he instructed my father to get his family out or did he assume that he would? My father is testifying about the series of dangerous incidents we've been involved in: the many times we've had to leave the house because of suspect bombs, the shooting attack when a woman was shot dead; the car engine that landed at our kitchen door when an explosion went off; the two close shaves when we tried to escape and the bombs went off in front of us.

'We got trapped,' I tell J, panic rising. 'I didn't know what to do.'

'Trapped,' J mused. 'This is a critical experience for you, isn't it? And there's your terror of being trapped in a sexual relationship.'

I can't hear him. 'You see, maybe it was my fault. Because I was in my nightdress, I had my period ...'

I have forgotten I have already told him this. I have assumed the polar-opposite position to silence and need to keep relentlessly going over this, excavating for meaning. How to make sense of this fused violent/sexual world pressing in, and me, paralysed with terror, unable to cross over into life? How to trust that J will understand what I cannot?

It was my father's refrain: 'You can do whatever you like when you're eighteen. Until then, you're living in my house under my rules.' After the bomb in 1975, there was a family vote about whether or not to go back to the dream house. Apparently I had emphatically voted no. Mummy too. Daddy had voted yes. Was it a case of no surrender, no one getting him out of his castle, his protest against the injustice of it all? So we went back.

At eighteen, I escaped to Dublin to study. The next bomb happened in the summer of 1980, at the end of my first year in college. When I returned to walk through the wrecked rooms and to hear the usual near-death stories, I felt a callous weariness. That night I stayed away. And the next.

By the Christmas of 1980 my parents were living in a mobile caravan on the tennis court while the dream house was being rebuilt once again. Then there was another bomb, and the mobile home got blown to bits. My parents rented another house, in another town, and lived there for a few years. And finally, when the older children had fled the North, my parents got a nice house, somewhere safe.

Just like that, with no seeming logic, the couch conversation angrily shifts to how I hate combined therapy, how furious I am with the group, accusing them of attacking me.

J adopts his directorial stance. 'This is not about the here and now. These are echoes of the past. The group is not doing anything to you. You are getting in touch with nerve ends, with feelings. Use the group and me to support you. Where was your mother when this turmoil was going on?'

'I don't know.'

It was Father who was the centre of my universe, Father who was Mother and Father at that time.

J urged, 'Tell the group about the terrible bomb. Trust the group.'

If I had told them at this juncture, you would have a story crafted with fictional coherence. However, an authentic therapeutic account is not that kind of linear narrative. It skates endlessly round on itself, spiralling in quirky cycles of progression and regression, boringly tracking the same old story, yet, each time around, understanding and meaning are being forged at deeper levels.

It was months before I could act on J's advice. In the meantime, for several nights, I pitched up late at my friend Nuala's flat. She did not know what was going on in therapy. She simply unpacked the sofa bed, made tea and said, 'You've always got a bed here for as long as you're frightened.'

4
Turning points

I am not I.
I am this one,
Walking beside me whom I do not see,
Whom at times I manage to visit,
And whom at other times I forget;

Juan Ramón Jiménez, 'I Am Not I', translated
by Robert Bly

IN JUNE 1990, the television series I had been research-ing was entering a summer recess. I worried about finding another contract that would pay enough to cover the cost of therapy. In the protracted couch silences, I felt criti cised for not bringing more stability to the process.

J commented, 'You've had a life of impermanence, haven't you? It's been hard for you to establish yourself, and you find yourself attracted to this environment of transience.'

Sunlight was filtering onto the couch when J asked in a tone of friendly curiosity, 'What makes your heart sing?'

He seemed to be suggesting that a singing heart was a morally acceptable option. From a long lost time ago, a lovely memory washed in.

My mother is in her classroom, her secret world. She is confident and happy here. Every afternoon when I finish primary school, I walk down to the secondary school where my parents teach. I sit at the back of my mother's room. These children are older than me. They have a special word: remedial. My mother loves them.

It's the annual making of the wall mural. My mother has been planning it for weeks, looking up art books, cutting out magazine pictures, jotting down ideas. We're to save our purple crinkly sweet papers for colour. The Wise Men's gifts are made from velvet, offered by the domestic-science teacher. There is a desert with sand which we collected from the river. Mummy is at her wall, drawing, painting, directing.

On the last day before Christmas holidays, we children stand back, sipping the celebratory orange juice she's bought for us. The mural is revealed. We clap, delighted with ourselves. My mother smiles over at me.

It was a delightful conversation, linking my love of the creative life with my treasured inner experience of 'the good mother', and, after that, I made a new choice. I took on a short-term contract to help establish an international children's film festival in Northern Ireland. The contract was supposed to last only four months, yet eventually my involvement blossomed into six years.

A new realm of professional creative happiness was opening up, one that paralleled the befriending of an internal world.

Every year, J's office closed for the month of August, and, in the lead-up to it, we would arrange an individual review session. Approaching my second summer, I am telling him how depressed I have been feeling.

'The therapy is deeper now. You are coming into contact with those raging, fearful parts of yourself from which you had turned away. Contact with these cut-off parts is helpful. It is actually a sign of health. Let's look at your repeating pattern: your constant crises, your inability to take the time to analyse ...'

I bristle, hearing an ungenerous tirade of blame heaped in my direction. A tide is inexorably pulling us out towards that familiar dynamic of closeness followed by conflict. I mutter something self-justifying and cross.

'You see me as rigid, yet I know the importance of these sessions for you,' J says. 'My respect shows itself in a pattern of dependability.' It is on the tip of my tongue to sling at him 'big bloody deal'. He goes on: 'You can't see me as an ally, a collaborator.' He sounds sad, not castigating. 'I'm on *your* side. Join with me in the analytic process. Disidentify from what is powerful.'

I recognise the word 'disidentify' from psychosynthesis – meaning to step back from fully identifying with my thoughts and feelings, to become more aware of myself as a thinker of thoughts, a feeler of feelings.

J makes a conciliatory peace offering, 'I am impressed with your commitment to therapy.' He adds a compassionate notion: 'What about the child who could not win her vote within the family, who could not have her hurt and terror? The child's experience of lack of democracy is being replayed in the room.'

A meeting ground has been found with that accurate interpretation. 'Perhaps you're coping better than you think,' J says. 'You are expanding your sense of identity, discovering that there is more to you than you originally thought. The child in you feels she will go hysterical. She is afraid of going mad.'

That is it exactly: the terror of being uncontainable, of losing my identity.

'You're not mad. You are coming close to the *original* feelings of anxiety, panic and fear. These things can be dealt with in here. You can work on developing a calm centre within.'

He is giving me a gift to hold on to during the August separation, the hope that I can create a new way of being *on the inside*, not have to keep on exhaustingly bolstering myself up on the outside.

J ends with the session with a thought-provoking statement: 'The call is to internalise the therapy.'

In that moment I understood him perfectly, but when I wrote up my journal in the evening, insight had once more run away.

'I want to practise loving in this room.'

I did not have the courage to articulate on the couch what I really meant: loving a man. *Loving you.*

J sounded puzzled.

'You can't practise loving. You can only love.'

'Do you think so?' I replied. Inside I thought, *Sure, it's just a little practice.*

There is a note in my diary, entered six months after starting combined therapy. 'Monday, 24 September 1990:

Turning point in the group.' However, there is no indication of what had happened.

Perhaps I had let J's words in: 'Are you seeking to control the therapy by taking these notes, trying to be a therapist to yourself? Surrender to the process. If it is important, you will remember it.'

Couch sessions are spent arguing over the group. According to J, my mind is hunting around for divisive issues to light upon, in order to stop me engaging with the painful ones emerging in therapy.

'The group has brought you back in touch with your humanity. Your identity is bound up with a suffering that makes you feel distinctive. The realisation that suffering is shared, that you're not special, makes you feel merged. We need to take time to explore the feelings that the group is shoring up for you. You're not the only one who struggles with relationships, you know.'

I tell J I am afraid of being quizzed about sexual relationships in the group. J insists he would pick up on anyone being voyeuristic, but he did not pick up when Damien started walking me back to my bus stop. When I told J on the couch, worried that the awkward situation was somehow my fault, he replied, 'Why this theme of punishment? Can't you take your portion of responsibility, not responsibility for everything? You don't have to assume the scapegoat role.'

But when the matter came up in the circle, J questioned, 'I am wondering what is happening that members are breaking my rules about no contact outside the group? Perhaps there is anger about me bringing someone new in?'

And, *bang*, I felt identified as the epicentre of the trouble, the intruder who has disrupted the cosy family order. That was when I thought that the status quo would be restored if I left.

On the couch you could be silent for extended periods but in the group somebody would invariably bat a question or a comment in your direction.

'You seem down.' It was Damien, the man with whom I was in entrenched dispute over feminism. The way he talked about 'birds' infuriated me, yet my lacerating zeal would have been unrecognisable to my friends. I hated how Damien kept zooming in on me, making me feel swamped and under siege. Often he would generate a conversation about sexual relationships, which I dreaded, my inability to reply making me feel even more visibly inadequate and threatened.

I summoned up my courage. 'I don't fit in here. I can't get the group "right". I want to leave.'

Damien was the first to respond, revealing his bear heart beneath the bluffing banter. 'Speaking for myself, I'd be sad if you left.'

Anna scooped me up with a good-mothering comment, 'I want to take you by the hand, bring you in. The group would be diminished by any of us leaving.'

Members were united. 'Stay. We'd miss you.'

For weeks, I had been fearful that J would refuse to work with me unless I revealed the most vulnerable aspects of myself in the group. Yet tonight everyone seemed to understand how afraid I was. No one put any pressure on me.

The talk turned to intimate relationships. I listened. The human journey was being revealed as complex and contradictory, where nothing was what it seemed. Fear, apparently, could drive people in diametrically opposite directions. I thought: *Maybe other people don't know what to do in relationships either; they muddle along as best they can.*

It was as J maintained: 'The group is a marvellous opportunity to learn about yourself and others; to explore and discover yourself.'

I looked around the group, and a new-moon thought sailed out from behind a fog: *J's not the common denominator.*

That was it. Until now, I had thought that such a disparate band could have met only through J. That gave J immense power. Now I realised that being human was the greater interconnecting force, and J was simply a part of that.

It was a wonderful conversation, and, if we could have sent out to the corner pub for glasses and a bottle of Bushmills and lit a turf fire in our wee snug of a circle, we would have done so. I do not think you are supposed to say this about group analysis, but the craic was good. There was laughter and sadness, regret and hope, loss and learning. There was an almost celebratory quality, as if something unifying had broken through and was cementing bonds. The more members spoke of their weaknesses and strengths in sexual relationships – this had mysteriously evolved into the evening's theme – the more confident I grew. I did not have to carry a leper's burden. J was right: 'The individual problem is the group problem.'

The group had come thrillingly alive in the connection that became possible if we could only edge out beyond our separate enclaves of fear, shame and isolation. Perhaps I could trust the group a smidgen.

'It is time.' J raised his hands. The time had flown. No one moved. If we stopped, this moment would die.

J sounded upbeat. 'We can continue our conversation next week.'

I remember nothing else of what J said; for once, a chink of space had been created for others. We trooped down the stairs afterwards, laughing at Damien, the court jester, who was carrying on. Anna turned to me at the door, 'See you next week.'

The evening I was going to concede defeat became when I really joined the group. The members had proved their willingness to accept me as I was; I did not have to sacrifice my individuality. From this point on, I would gloriously sail forth and enjoy the group experience.

Three weeks later, I went back to bickering.

The major threat to my therapy happened in the autumn of 1990. Then again, if it had not been for this incident, something else would have occurred, for, as J used to repeat, re-enactment is inevitable in therapy. Situations from an *earlier* time, he stressed, would be re-experienced, providing an opportunity for the original wounds to be seen, known and worked through.

It was a challenge when a friend wanted to become one of J's patients, which happened about four times during the course of my therapy. My reluctance seemed morally wrong when there were few good, trained psychotherapists in Northern Ireland. I couldn't wail 'I need him for me.'

When my friend told me of her negotiations with J, I was shocked. She had informed J that it would be impossible to meet during the daytime so, after two meetings, they had agreed to a 6.30 p.m. session.

For two years I had been waiting for an evening session. Four months previously, the holy grail of a permanent arts position had come up, based outside Belfast.

'Is there any chance of an evening session?'

Since J's answer had been 'no', I had withdrawn as a candidate. Therapy with J was the most important commitment in my life.

Now I would not accept J's questions as a form of answer.

'I am willing to reply in a moment but I'm wondering ...? What comes into your mind when you say ...?'

I won't budge: 'Is there or isn't there an evening waiting list?'

Eventually, he replies warily, 'No, there isn't one.'

When the storm breaks, he asks a good question: 'Why do you imagine I offered the time to her and not to you?'

My answer comes easily, 'Because I don't matter, do I?' And if he had known her for longer, I might have slipped into my riff, 'because you love her more, because she gets everything I want, because she's prettier than me ...'

J had previously offered guidance about managing the transition from couch to outer world. ('Leave everything with me.') It was a relief to hand over my intensity to someone else.

On summer days he might add, reinforcing the principles of right perspective and right balance, 'Everything doesn't have to be sorted today. Go on out and enjoy this weather.' I would hear his Zen encouragement: love life. In winter, he might remark, 'This too will pass. Everything changes, like the sun and the clouds. The light will come back, and so will the dark.'

However, whenever he and I had fallen out, I would spend the entire weekend crying.

The Monday-morning room contracts in stoniness. J speaks first, 'Can we look at what might be being re-evoked from the past?'

'No.'

If J holds to his theory that this is re-enactment, I feel denied the present-day reality of his abominable behaviour. I will not let him defend himself with his sleek analytic armoury.

'Well then, let's talk about termination of your therapy.'

Touché. He has played his trump card, reinforcing it with that callous professional term. Off with her head.

His manner denotes 'I have no personal investment in you. I don't need your money. I am the King of the Castle. You either play by my rules or you don't play at all.'

I respond, 'I can't talk about that. [*Silence.*] I can't stay if there's no trust. [*Long silence.*] You know, I rang my friend Jane. She reminded me of something. She said, he's always been there for you, every step of the way; he's never let you down.'

'I am glad for you that you have Jane.'

He values someone I love, the one person prepared to stand up for him. He goes on, 'I think the group is needed to offer balm, as Jane has done. She has acted in the tradition of the interceding mother, hasn't she? Could we open up this wound?'

The 'wound' is one of his favourite words.

I begrudgingly offer, 'It's something to do with trust. I want to trust you – to trust in therapy – but I can't.'

'That's the same as wanting to be happy, yet being sad. You keep hiding from the darker side of yourself, protecting it. As for this degree of sensitivity ...'

Will he call me the Princess and the Pea, the Tragedy Queen, as he does in the group, puncturing and hurting me?

'... you have taken this incident as a personal slight. The truth is I didn't think about anyone.'

Stab of hurt: he didn't think about me.

'... I saw your friend because she was a friend of yours. I constructed a session to see how it could be managed. It's not a hanging offence.'

He sounds angry, as if I have manoeuvred him into a hateful, wrong-footed place. He comments, not without regret, 'It would always have ended in betrayal. I cannot be what you want me to be. I cannot give you what you want me to give. To the outside world, this must seem a strange relationship, to have such dependence on someone you only see three times a week. But we both know it's not *really* me, is it? It's who I've come to represent. It's connected to *internal*, not external, reality.'

He drives home analytic nails.

'... What trust was broken in the family? What was the original act of betrayal? What was going on that the child was hurting herself?' Finally, reiterating that combined therapy is one integrated process, he suggests, 'Bring this to the group. See what they have to say.'

I have a faded piece of paper, a freeze-frame of one group meeting, because, afterwards, I wrote up my own detailed notes. Ever dramatic (*melodramatic*, J – accurately – counters), I claim the opening minutes. J makes no comment. Ideally I would like people to chime in unison, 'That's an awful thing he's done.' It is the first time I am going to Mummy for help.

The first reaction is Tom's. 'What a mountain out of a molehill.' His scorn implies, 'I don't understand a word you're on about, woman.' Tom and I have been locked in a tango of negative attacks. There is an element embedded in Tom's story, which resonates with a shadow part of mine, threatening me in ways I cannot allow myself to consciously know. So each week we assume battlefield positions, make sniping strikes, mirror hated secret bits of self to the other, oblivious to the sideline murmurs, 'What's *really* going on here?' We are twins, forged from the same miserable psychological fire and, hidden within the embers, as J has noticed, is an unspoken affection.

Mary is next. Even-tempered and reasonable, she is the elder sister figure with whom I negatively compare myself. 'You've a sense of panic about this. You were grateful for what you had until you saw what somebody else had. Then you wanted that.'

The others are joining in with a range of responses, for this is therapy by the group of the group, and there are nine therapists in the room.

'It's the Prodigal Son scenario, isn't it? You're the loyal, committed one, upstaged by somebody else. It's your envy for the fatted calf your friend has been offered.'

Only Damien pitches in with the longed-for outrage. 'Jesus Christ, isn't he a fucking cowboy?' A first-class reaction. Buy that man a drink.

J does not react throughout the toing and froing.

Anna speaks next: 'J has been accommodating to me. I would need to hear his side before I could comment. It's two extremes, isn't it? On the one hand, there's a professional relationship and, on the other, this idealistic aspect where you want it to be much more. Is this about forgiveness, what is forgivable? You seem to be attributing great significance to these events, as though it were a test. You know, like, "he loves me, he loves me not".'

The invisible baton is being passed around the members.

'Is it about sharing J, realising he has many clients, you're not the only one? The time factor of sessions is an important element, but it's not that important.'

Mary goes on to relate how she is working hard to put her relationship with J on an adult footing. I think, *Why can't I be at that hallowed grown-up stage, instead of being the frustrated child whom everyone wants to be older, more able than I am?* Their reactions culminate in a question: 'What do you want? Isn't it enough that J has acknowledged his role?'

'I want an evening session.'

Someone interjects, 'Oh no, I don't think it's fair to ask for that.'

I reiterate the stress of protecting sessions, when therapy is alien to my working culture and I can be called away at any moment. I am not like other members who run their own companies or who do not have to work, or who are in social-work-type jobs, where therapy has been openly negotiated.

The musing continues from the chorus. They are giving me time and space – valuable premiums – with which they could be working on their own troubles. I have the attention of Group Mother, not quite 'There, there,' but a mediating force, helping J and me out of deadlock.

'Is this connected to the child knowing she'll never be loved by the parents the way she loves and needs them? Is it about wanting to be loved?'

The group wants me to forgive J. I can't. I find myself drawn to talking about the fractured ley lines in my story: the sequence of bombs, the mistake we made in going back to the house, not being able to communicate with my mother. J is commenting that I am working through deeply painful material: not feeling safe with men, being repeatedly placed in dangerous situations.

As he is eliciting possible levels of meanings, Tom lashes across him. 'Honestly, what does this matter?' He turns on me. 'I'm annoyed with you. This is ridiculous.'

'This matters,' I insist stubbornly, 'to me.'

Tom glares. This is how it is between us.

Damien rounds on me too. 'I find it hard to concentrate when what you're saying is rich. You're too much.'

J is intervening again, inviting people to take back their own destructiveness, rather than projecting it out for others to carry.

Miriam has the last word to me. 'I envy you. You're lucky to be in therapy with J' – she smiles at him – 'when you're young and have life ahead of you. Whatever the problem is, I am sure you and J will work it out.'

Ironically, the next couch session had been arranged for 9.20 p.m., in order to accommodate my work schedule. J did not have to meet late in the evening, but he did. Even so, all I could think, trekking up the stairs, was, *Has the bedrock of our relationship – trust – been betrayed? Have I come to the end of the road with therapy? Why do the people I love let me down?*

Daddy wants us to see a psychiatrist, to go for compensation from the government. 'What if you ever blamed me in later life, for not taking you out of the house the night the bomb went off? I couldn't bear it if you were ever angry with me. If you get compensation, I'll tell myself, you'll know I did my best for you.'

I must never feel angry, or sad, or upset. Emotions are frightening. I love my father, and he loves me. He needs me to do this for him. Happiness is best. Unspoken guilt and grief hover like desolate black birds.

The two male psychiatrists work in the hospital, known locally as the loony bin. I'm fifteen. It is like being interviewed for a job. Or interrogated. At first it's easy. Name. Age. School. The older one is looking at his notes. 'We understand you were menstruating that night, one of your first periods. Could you tell us about that?'

I want the whole world to swallow me up. Tears of humiliation are welling. They've sent me in, unprotected. Either individually or jointly, they've told these men about the intimacies they can't even broach with me. What can I do as they grill me about whether my

95

menstruation has been affected: regular, flow, cycle, light, heavy. The psychiatrists want me to talk about explosions, loud noises and warning sirens. I can't. I long to escape these persecutors, to go back to the house where people are honest enough to want someone dead.

Blow me away. The pain will be over quickly.

Mummy and Daddy look anxious as I climb into the car. Silence is the one punishing weapon I possess. Everywhere is worry. A mortgage company pursuing payments for a house we can't even live in, applications for emergency housing turned down, insensitive letters from a government assessor, a second rented house that Daddy has to pay for. No one cares about us in this hostile world. No one is to be trusted. Look at those men who pitched in to help on the night of the explosion. They said 'Sorry for your troubles.' Later it emerged that they had planted the bomb. The sly Trojan horse, the strategy of ignoble war. Former pupils from my parents' school. Catholics like us.

So, anger – that seething, nail-packed explosive – is pushed down into the pit of a thing called body. The bomb was the horrendous event wasn't it? But the meeting with the psychiatrists felt much more devastating. It felt like an intimate act of betrayal, effected by people who loved me and whom I loved and needed desperately.

J and I were facing into the night test of our alliance, straining in a bloodied and hurt place. He said he wanted to understand what had been happening in the therapy, in service of me, of our work together. He was prepared to take responsibility for his part in the misunderstanding.

'I wasn't taking on any new patients. You had asked for my help. That was the only reason I met your friend.'

I heard his good intention: that he cared enough about me to make an exception. Around the evening session, he seemed to be indicating that he had made a mistake. And, just like that, my inner sky lit up. J was not going to indulge in any of the excoriating behaviour that he had been pointing out to me for months: being hard on myself, beating myself up. He was human. It did not mean the end of our work – far from it, he assured me.

'This *is* the work. The edifice of the therapy can hold up.'

Through the precision of his vocabulary, I heard J communicating that he knew how terrible it was to drag around an internal collapsing world. He understood that talking about the house collapsing on top of me was also a symbolic attempt at conveying another, much earlier, terrifying experience of *internal* collapse, and the two were impossibly enmeshed in my unconscious. He talked about the 'strength of our foundations', our 'structural solidity', and I felt hope rising. Our relationship did not have to be destroyed as everything had been before.

A mistake was not the same as a betrayal. Rage did not necessarily mean the death of love; indeed, rage and love could be connected.

You could love and fight someone, forge a language for conflicting feelings – something I had never found possible in my family – and how liberating that was. J and I could tussle with each other, and hate each other, but we could also hang on in there. The worst of situations was redeemable with a change of perspective. Life was not fixed or perfect; it did not need to be. Equally important was what J had said – a bit sheepish, mind – after our dogged commitment to the work that meant so much to both of us.

'Well, now, a session has become available on Thursdays at 5 p.m. I am offering it to you first.' He was backing up his words with action.

And this was how I knew, for the first time, of the value of combined therapy, because it was the group that had helped us to survive and, astonishingly, to triumph.

J weaves a nest of understanding with his repeating phrases. 'I know this is distressing for you ... These difficulties have formed over many years and will take time to change ... Can you be gentle, be patient with yourself? ... You will never undertake any journey as hard as this again.'

Deepening trust means that he can lead me back to the unbearable material that refuses to go away.

'Were you trying to stop growing up?'

How can he be imaginatively forgiving, when the truth is that there is no explanation to the self-hurting teenage rituals?

'Were you trying to punish someone?'

If only I could assign words to these resurfaced experiences but I cannot find the monumental courage necessary, although I try and try.

'Were you acting out what you thought had been done to you?'

Recently, a man my own age had asked me out. The sick panic had started up as soon as the relationship had become physical. It had ended within a fortnight.

The rain through the window never stops as my tears drip onto the listening couch. 'I'm the walking wounded, damned to eternal terror, incapable of loving anyone. I feel a failure after two years of therapy. I keep thinking of a prayer my mother taught me as a child: "Sacred Heart of Jesus, I place all my trust in Thee".'

'What do you need?'

J's quiet question implies an abiding faith in me to know the answer inside myself, beyond the outer emotional chaos.

Eventually I reply, 'Don't leave me alone with this.'

His hand-on-heart commitment is that he will *be* with me.

'Jesus, there's not a single female image in here. I'm surrounded by nothing but bloody men.'

Three distinguished figures peer over the couch. Sigmund Freud, a solemn face, is captured in a pen portrait. Carl Jung, a fine profile, is an etching. Roberto Assagioli is a smiling photograph. Finally, there is the fourth man, himself in the chair behind.

No comment.

'I'm sure you all have a good laugh at me. Box me in with your theories. You don't know what it's like to be struggling to become a woman.'

Now I am getting on my subtly-undermining-him-as-a-therapist wheel.

'How on earth can you work with women in such a male room? Do you mean to tell me there are no female therapists you admire?'

Maybe I have hit a nerve because J sounds arch. We are getting stuck in.

'Whom or what do you suggest?'

Out of nowhere shuffles my winning ace: 'Where the hell is Melanie Klein?'

I have read not one word by Melanie Klein, know sod-all about the woman, but I have picked up that she is an influential figure in psychoanalysis. She'll do. The disgrace that this gifted woman should be treated shabbily! Mournful shake of head; words fail me.

Some time later, I noticed something different about the wall. Then it dawned on me that a small fourth portrait had been added, a black-and-white photograph of a severe, rather off-putting woman. Beside her was a girl, a daughter perhaps, although they did not seem close. The older, unsmiling woman emanated tremendous guts and steel. And I just knew. *It was Melanie Klein.* She had made it to the analysts' wall. She was up there, in her own right, amidst those towering men.

He had heard. He had responded.

Margaret Thatcher has resigned as prime minister. I wonder how J will react for our conversations can open anywhere, culminating in 'And is there any connection between this and what is happening in the therapy?'

However, pinned to his door are two notes: one for the group he must be working with later, and one for me. His hasty fountain pen reads something like: 'My wife has been taken into hospital. I've had to leave to be with her. So sorry.'

Afraid that any gesture I make will be overanalysed to death, I slip a note under his door, saying if I can help he only has to ask. I do not know how to show that I care for him. It is later that it occurs to me that maybe it is a happy event, like having another baby.

Forty-eight hours later I am at the theatre with friends. A man has joined us.

(*'My wife'*)

I will call him Peter. During the interval, Peter sits beside me.

(*'To be with her.'*)

I have heard a lot about him. He has an attractive face, a relaxed intelligence and an air of integrity.

(*'My wife'*)

I think I have decided to fall in love with *another* man, to go for something *real*, although this thought is not conscious. It is only writing this that I understand.

J is formidable on Greek and Roman mythology, referring to obscure gods, of whom no one else could possibly have heard. He loves poetry (Dante, Keats, Yeats, be prepared for a lot of boring T.S. Eliot) and classical literature (Shakespeare, Blake) – definitely not the contemporary American work I admire, since anything American is open to his snorting derision. He likes to murmur, 'you young people today' and 'modern-day relationships' with a faintly dismissive sigh, looking down woefully on the mess that is the late twentieth century. Sometimes he waxes, 'Anyone, the birds and beasts in the fields, can have sex. It is a basic animal instinct. It is not about a mature, intimate relationship.' Each time, I think wistfully, *I wish I were a bird.*

He is brilliant on the panoply of Oedipal desire, transference and counter-transference, although he never refers to them by these elevated terms. But is he of this planet at all, and does he know anything about kissing and dating and what a woman is supposed to do with a man? That would be handy now. Because Peter's card – chorus of angels singing! – has arrived, asking if we could meet again.

5

First love

The bud
stands for all things,
even for those things that don't flower,
for everything flowers, from within, of self-blessing;

Galway Kinnell, 'Saint Francis and the Sow'

I AM so happy to be dating a lovely man and not feel sick with fear that I could fling my arms around J in gratitude. Instead, we enact the psychoanalytic version of rampant ecstasy: we shake hands.

Back in the office, my colleague lights a cigarette. 'Are you off to see your boyfriend in Dublin this weekend?'

The art is to hit the right, carefree tone in response, as if you have had a tiresome supply of lovers all your life.

'Yeah, my boyfriend' – shimmering, sultry sounds – 'is meeting me tomorrow night.'

On our first date, Peter and I went to see *An Angel at My Table*, and there was the pleasure of a fine film combined with the bliss of being normal, being like ordinary people out on a Saturday-night date.

J and I had already talked about sexual attraction, another on my interminable list of insecurities. I mean, how did you know you were attracted to someone? What if you made a mistake and then could not get out of it because the other person might feel betrayed? J asked, 'You know that pitter-patter sensation in the base of your stomach?'

I had been afraid to let on that I felt nothing in the stone-body, that what was obviously free-flowing for him was not for me. Yet here was a sensitive, good-hearted man (I mean Peter) with whom I felt safe, partly because I recognised a vulnerability that was similar to my own.

J perked up when I told him that Peter and I had *really* kissed. Previously, I would have been so worried about managing what-was-coming-next that a kiss in itself could not be enjoyed.

'How was that for you?' J asked.

'It was great,' I replied, remembering how Peter had stroked my hair and how our mouths meeting was an enjoyable sensation – not a pitter-patter, but certainly a pitter. We were two people who had miraculously found each other and were going to take our relationship slowly.

For two years, J had steadfastly kept open the avenues to the impossible: finding a language in which to talk about intimacy and sexuality. He was growing into his craft, no longer interjecting too early with 'Afraid of ...?' when 'I'm afraid ...' needed to flutter in the room like a Tibetan prayer flag, feeling the weight of itself in the wind. He was learning to trust that the hieroglyphic fragments were the best I could do, that I was trying to communicate a terror that was real but without any seeming meaning, something that needed time to emerge, and the form of the telling was part of the message.

Earlier, I had managed to tell J about a night I had spent with a male friend, whom I had first met four days after Carmel's funeral, during that sessionless Easter void, when my body had gone insane and was craving the touch I could not get from J.

I had been cutting tape in the office, and my hand was trembling. This new colleague had come over, said 'Let me help you,' and had put his hand on mine.

A friendship had developed over months, although the lines delineating the exact nature of the relationship were not clear. One evening after several intimate conversations, the suggestion of lovemaking had materialised in my friend's house. The man did not know of my sexual inexperience, because I could not tell him – this was part of the ghastly anxiety, the pressure of having to hide. Somehow (these things would be as blurry in the retelling as they were at the actual time) we had taken off our clothes.

I was visible, and so was he – the first man I had seen naked. As the prospect of lovemaking crushed in, the worst of the panic had walloped me. I had begun crying, body shaking, feeling petrified.

My friend had been taken aback, but he was decent. 'We don't have to do this. We can have a cup of tea.' It was then that I remembered J's worrying comment: could

I, unconsciously, be creating the very situations where rape might become possible, only, thankfully, choosing men who would not do it?

This had flummoxed me, so could J explain the rules? How did a woman pace a healthy sexual relationship with a man?

'I'm afraid of the penis,' I mumbled on the couch.

Jesus, could I not be more original? Did I have to be so frigging Freudian? But I was practising the explicit vocabulary that J had been evenly voicing, experiencing what it was like to reveal the shameful truth to a man and feeling his unmitigating honesty in return.

The penis was merely a bodily appendage, J had airily replied. I argued no, that it represented male power. The voice behind the couch exclaimed in delight, 'Ah, the penis is beautiful!'

'Yeah,' I drawled, 'bet you're saying that because you've got one.'

And so our conversations quickened, skipped, and then stalled.

J and I explored the possibility that I might be a lesbian. This did not have the same energy as the jumbled-up confusion of wanting but not wanting to be attractive to a man. I had been born into the wrong century, I mournfully informed J. This was the tragic myth I needed to cling to. I should have been living in the nineteenth century, where men courted from afar, where there was romance without sex, and where tyrannical fathers vetted dashing suitors.

'You mean the century with the highest level of child prostitution and poverty?' J challenged.

Slowly, slowly, a shape moulded from the going-to-die panic: the fantasy of a man trapped inside my body in the act of sexual intercourse and me reduced to unbearable powerlessness.

J started going over a pragmatic theme, as if he was drumming in an understanding that might stand me in good stead: 'You can say "no" at any stage in sex. It doesn't matter, at whatever point, if it's not right for you, you say "no".'

And I felt moved – although I did not know why – that a man was telling me, a woman, that I had a right to my no. But it made no difference to my terror-driven anxiety.

It is the last couch session before my third Christmas in therapy, in 1990. My fragile self feels nourished by the richness of J's interpretations.

'You have been struggling with this powerful, sickening feeling, the toxic within, wrestling with difficulties in intimacy, similar to those you experience in the group.'

The group had continued on its gruelling trajectory, culminating in me walking home afterwards, in tears.

'You reacted to "playing hard to get" and "tease" on an absolutist level, rather than hearing the overall sense.'

That is what two men in the group had accused me of. I had felt cut to the bone as the group's only single (i.e. 'available') woman. I was unforgiving with the other women who had stayed quiet when I had asked for support, and with J, who questioned what underlay my 'superficial' outrage. I felt set up and hung out to dry as the group's stereotypical feminist: afraid of men, rejecting men, not delivering what a good woman should.

Two days later, midway through Thursday's couch session, J is on a roll. 'The group was saying that it is hard – not impossible – to get into a close relationship with you. What about asking people what they mean rather than assuming the worst? You foresee suffering, and it can become a self-fulfilling prophecy, projecting the past into the future. Maybe the men needed to hear from a woman that dividing women into the madonna and the whore isn't appropriate.'

I feel annoyed. Why did he leave me to take the fire at the time?

'Your central experience is of being trapped. You have this repeating fantasy of being trapped with a man, of coercion against your will in the group, in therapy. It's not true. You are free to go at any time.'

He is right.

'You've made a success out of your career. You're not a passive woman. You're beautiful and talented. Despite the odds, you have generated creative opportunities for yourself and others.'

Could we go back to *beautiful*?

'You make me think of my own daughters. There is the sense of a father needing to give time to his daughter.'

My heart feels warmed.

'What about the child's terror of being trapped, of not being in control, being dependent on the adults? The child alone in her bedroom with sharp objects?'

I don't want to hear this. I want to hold on to the 'happy' me.

'Talk to the group about the pain inside.'

I can't.

'You've had supreme courage to undertake this journey and stick at it. Now it's time to relax and enjoy the Christmas holidays. There has been emotional turmoil, but you've made great strides. Things have changed in the external world. The therapy is progressing well.'

That feels good.

From the moment I met Peter, I promised myself that I would do everything within my power to stop the age-old terror corroding the possibility of a good relationship. That meant risking more in therapy, trusting that J would not judge my fears. As the relationship with Peter developed, transfixing panic took the form of a terror of pregnancy.

J sought to ascertain what degree of sexual intimacy was taking place. He talked about erections. I did not have the couch confidence to ask him, 'Um, could we go through the basics?'

So we would drift across that vast plain, a Roman Catholic upbringing. I would remember my mother warning me never to get into bed with a boy, and me coming up with more and more ludicrous situations: what if there was a fire in the house, and the beds got burned, and the only place to sleep was with a boy? The answer was consistently 'no'.

I remembered being about ten years old and the radio announcing that Bernadette Devlin, the youngest woman ever to be elected to the Westminster Parliament, had had a child out of marriage. The mood at the kitchen table was one of disappointment.

An intergenerational cultural attitude towards sexuality revealed itself on the couch.

I found myself transferring the experience of speaking about intimate matters from one setting to another. I was able to tell Peter about my sexual inexperience and was met with an understanding response. One burden felt lifted.

Damien advised me to let go of the 'hang-ups of equality', that I would be better off becoming a 'seductive woman with wiles'. The group consensus seemed to be that it was 'masculine' to not want marriage and 'natural' for a woman to have children. Everyone agreed, including – he could not deny it, I saw him nodding – J.

J took it upon himself to remind the group that I had entered therapy because of difficulties with sexuality, problems, he said, with being a woman. It was the first time I realised that J saw his role as telling me how to be a woman.

I felt hemmed in: either I had to conform to the group norm (which I regarded as sexist and traditional) or face rejection. That night, I wrote to J:

Letter extract, 28 February 1991
You cannot teach me to be a woman. You are a man, and, no matter what you say, I know more about being a woman than you do. All I wanted you to offer was a safe, secure, caring environment to explore my own sexuality and womanhood so that I would come to the truth of my femaleness, as *I* want to express it, not as you or the group or

society would like me to. Whether that was your intention or not, you have helped me do this. I have grown immensely as an individual and, per se, as a woman. I can see, however, that the group offers no such cultural freedom.

You could be party to situations in combined therapy that would never be possible in either individual therapy or group therapy. In individual therapy, the work takes place between the patient and the therapist, in group therapy within the confines of a group, but in combined therapy these lines criss-cross in complex and subtle ways.

Two women members were ending their respective therapies, and both had decided to leave the group on the same night. I had never participated in a leave-taking before, so was heartened to hear how therapy had revitalised two different lives. Only J's elliptical comment at the end baffled me: 'Now your therapy begins.'

One of the women, Mary, had been working with J for five years, and she had mentioned in the group that her final individual session was due to take place before my Thursday one. So afterwards, in a couch session, I had suggested to J that we could reschedule our usual Thursday meeting for the day of Mary's departure.

'What is your fantasy about the leaving process?' J had asked me.

Ideally, I wanted him to be distraught, but sad would do – just to give any indication of a personal impact.

'You love me with the passionate intensity of a young child,' J replied sternly. 'You want me to love you in the same way. We will meet at the usual time.'

On the day of Mary's leaving, I sat upright on the couch and proceeded to boldly scrutinise J's face. After several minutes, I dismissively summed him up. 'Mary's leaving hasn't made the slightest difference to you, has it?'

He stared back coolly. Eventually he replied, in a sharp, upbraiding tone. 'You haven't learnt the difference between the interior and exterior, have you? Between what you see on the surface and know in your heart?'

The truth of what he was saying sank in, as did the surprising realisation that I had hurt him.

Then he did something most unusual. He stood up – the impact of breaking the cloistered order of our universe – and walked over to the window. He stood gazing out for what felt like a long time, his back to me. When he spoke (he did not turn around), he sounded tired. 'Maybe a break would be good.' It was the first time he had ever indicated his own willingness to give up. For weeks I had been flinging at him, 'You're sick of me. We should take a break.'

He had consistently replied, 'I'm not weary of you. I am willing to travel the journey with you.'

Our work was teetering on the verge of collapse, ending not with melodramatic shrieks but with the subdued tragedy of neither of us being able to bring the therapy to a resolution, no matter how hard we tried. The unconscious had won out.

Sadness halted my pseudo-arguing.

'I don't know how to get less caught up here,' I said, 'how to be less impetuously aggressive. I want to be loving and warm, but we only seem capable of hurting each other.'

Then something happened. It was as if J had been making his own choice, because when he next spoke – having rooted himself in his therapist's chair again – it was with the note of grace descending. 'I trust you.'

It was such a beautiful, unexpected gift, one that caught me unaware. In the middle of our wrangling, I felt a purity of respect soaring back to him.

'I trust you too,' I said.

When he next spoke, I did not hear him blaming me, as it often felt. 'Your difficulties with the group are symptomatic of the difficulties within you. They are representative of your inner world. The problem is not with the group. It's the group *within you*, projected onto the group outside you.'

This was a hard concept to grasp, that the group could be a living theatre of the *internal* world.

'You are capable of relationships. You have potential.'

This was the same man who never failed to point out my intolerance and self-absorption.

'J, how can you say that when there's no evidence?'

'You *can* love. I can see it in the group.'

His unwavering faith in me never fails to move me. He adds poignantly, 'Working with Mary was five years of my life too.'

God, I am foolish. He cares about Mary, the group, maybe even about me.

'Ending is the most important aspect of therapy. Can you trust my judgement when it's a good time for someone to leave, that I can end properly?'

The truth was that Mary's leave-taking had prefigured the thought of my own some day, triggering a heaving separation anxiety.

'We are at a crossroads. We must let things settle until they become clearer.'

And, in the clearing ground of the following weeks, we both decided that it was not the right hour to take a break.

I do not remember now what my dream was about, but after J and I had let it wash over the two of us, J counselled, 'Listen to what your dream is telling you. You are not ready for sexual intercourse.'

It seemed astonishing that a dream could *know* me, and equally astonishing was our increased capacity to talk about intimate matters. I was learning that communication skills could be acquired, that I did not have to be all alone in an insecure-making world.

At first I felt disappointment, believing sexual intercourse to be the ultimate test that I would have to pass in order to prove to myself – to J – that I was well. Any sense of having an innate natural desire, of being able to relax into and trust my own female body, felt irretrievably shattered. Then I experienced an inflow of relief, heard the dream and J reassuring me, 'It's OK not to be ready.'

J was steering me through a first sexual relationship, protecting me from going too far when I was not ready in my body or psyche, supporting me to enjoy small steps. It was one of those rare times when I trusted myself. I chose to listen to the wisdom of my dream and to J's helpful interpretation, which reverberated with my own inner truth.

And, afterwards, I was eternally grateful.

In the Alice-in-Wonderland world of the couch, it is possible to fly across time zones in a fifty-minute time-travel machine. One day, J asks, 'What are you thinking?'

I realise that I am thinking a thought. It is about the Gaeltacht, that Irish-speaking part of the Republic where we teenage Northern Catholics went to learn Irish and where you had your best chance of a first kiss.

Silence. Silence.

J says, 'There is always a way in to talk. Rather than getting caught up with the content, you can liberate yourself by being curious about the process, by reflecting how it is that this incident can't be talked about, by exploring the thoughts, feelings and associations that stop you from speaking.'

A Kerry landscape is opening up in my mind.

Summer school. Maybe fourteen or fifteen. Staying with older Belfast girls who wear make-up and tell dirty jokes. Feel a bit afraid. Boys are in the classrooms here. Belfast boy sits in front of me. He turns around: 'Are you going to the ceilidh *on Friday night?' I feel shy, pleased. Belfast girl says, 'He fancies you.' She tells the others. They're impressed. I've passed some kind of test.*

And then ... you see, two days later ... I'm sitting in the kitchen of the bean an tí – *the woman of the house. Been worried sick all day. I'm telling her, I've got to go home. She says, 'You're getting on so well here, the* ceilidh's *tomorrow night, you'll enjoy that. If something's bothering you ...' For one second I think, 'Could I tell her what's happened?' My courage gets swept away.*

Mummy and Daddy are cross when they arrive to collect me. Sure, it's hundreds of miles' drive and they'd only left me there six days before. I don't say anything. I know I've failed at my one chance for freedom. From then on, it's the family joke. Whenever I want to do anything adventurous, someone will pipe up, 'Ah, it'll be like the Gaeltacht and you'll be back.'

Onto the couch sweeps the loneliness of never being able to tell anyone what is troubling me, and the punishing, fixating thought of how the whole of my life might have been different if even one coming-of-age ceremony had gone well. Consecutive sessions are punctuated by my murmurings: 'It's stupid ... I'm ridiculous ... Pathetic.'

J says, 'Can you observe how traumatic this incident is for you, how you still can't talk about it fourteen years later?'

His invitation is to take a step back and create a moment of awareness.

'Yes.'

But no words will form to tell him what had happened.

It is a Sunday afternoon in April 1991 when Peter says he needs to end our relationship, that he is sorry for presenting it like a bombshell.

On the Monday morning couch, I cry my heart out. I know I am not like those grown-up people who come to J with the real bone marrow of relationships: marriages, divorces and affairs. What touches me is J's valuing of my minuscule four-month-old relationship.

'This is the first time you've had your heart broken in this way, isn't it?' J says tender-heartedly. 'You've re-joined the human race.'

He asserts that what Peter and I have shared has had integrity, is an experience I can bring forward to the future, that two people can help each other, even if love does not ultimately flourish. He says that the life-enhancing aspect of this relationship has been stronger than the death anxiety, which sounds grand, except I sort of know what he means.

What were those words he used that first day I came to see him? Bifocal vision. This feels like a vision in action. He knows that this experience has been pivotal to my blossoming as a woman, so he will not collude with me when I downplay its importance, as a form of self-protection. He conveys the sense, 'If this matters to you, then it matters to me,' as though he is signalling, 'because *you* matter to me.'

'It must be hard to go back to work today.' He sounds sympathetic.

Normally I am merely required to cope with the strenuous demands of therapy. Next week I will be away at a week's psychosynthesis course, so there will be no sessions with J. He says that he too will be in Dublin at the weekend and offers the security of a meeting there. We can meet at Eckhart House.

So here we are, on a Saturday evening, in another city, removed from the boundaried safety of the couch.

For months J had been intoning, 'You don't want me to bring in the reality of the therapist–patient relationship. You write these letters, which are important attempts to communicate, yet you sign them "love" and add a kiss. You don't treat me like a therapist, more like a surrogate lover, father, friend.'

'Well, tell me how to relate to a therapist and I'll give it a go.'

But, in the unfamiliar Dublin environment, the association of an affair emerges. I tell him how part of me longs for – the squirming embarrassment – a loving relationship with him. I cannot look at him, worried in case he might think I am questioning his professional ethics.

'Can you let yourself play with these fantasies?'

'Play' makes things worse. I reveal that I had felt torn between him and Peter. My heart was not spacious enough for two men, and J dominated my inner world.

'You see, I'm so grateful to you. You've helped me change my concept of myself. I feel capable of working at a loving relationship. That's an amazing change. But – and I can't make sense of this – you're like a prison I feel trapped in, controlling and owning me. I feel I'll never be free.'

I like to study the colour and detail in J. On a good couch day, I gush to J that the Taj Mahal could not be as striking as his compassion; on a bad couch day J drawls that no therapist could meet my idealised demands.

My favourite shirt of his is a crisp pink-with-a-hint-of-purple one, which seems a radical, almost trendy choice for a classicist whose sole attire is three-piece suits. I also like his smart beige raincoat until I notice that his buttons preen *Yves Saint Laurent*. So that is where my hard-earned money is going.

His life seems busy. One evening, he gives a brilliant exposition about the value of play. Then, as the group ends (at 8.30 p.m.), the buzzer goes. So much for play, I think, that man is still working. He is superb on the importance of self-care, yet one summer he has such a terrible cough that I wonder would he not be better off looking after himself. I leave a miniature bottle of whiskey outside his door, in case a wee dram might help.

What I love about J is his personality, the way he does not deny dilemmas and scrapes – he works with them all the time – but still exudes the inspirational message that life is worth living and worth living well.

What drives me mad about him is his personality, the way he can be infuriatingly dismissive. He regularly calls my feminism 'facile' or a 'trip'. Anything I am interested in or knowledgeable about – the media or contemporary culture – he seems to dislike, although he tries to disguise this. One day, he makes a casual comment in that triangle of couch–coat–door as he watches me bundling *The Guardian* into my bag. 'I don't know how you can read that newspaper, with its typographical errors.'

He utters this at a time I want him to be as close to me as my shadow. Then I hit on a genius idea. *I can become him.* It is hard getting used to reading *The Independent*, after years of worshipping at the shrine of *The Guardian*. Yet, it is *The Independent* that J tucks under his coat when he strides up the stairs on Monday mornings. My one consolation is that J and I now share the same unified worldview. For weeks I sprinkle couch references to articles in *The Independent* or refer to the views of our mutual 'friend', the newspaper's Middle East correspondent, Robert Fisk, hoping that J might warmly respond.

He never says a word.

I became consumed with the fear that J might die – a terrible thought, for our fates were interlocked, like mother and baby. At night I had the same nightmare. I would be in a warren of streets, carrying a baby I knew to be my baby (this image never seemed odd), unable to remember which road led to J's office. The dream would be swelling into a crescendo of tension – *I'm not going to find him* – when he would appear. He would coldly bark 'You're late' or 'Your time's over,' or 'I've sold your session to someone else.' So to reach his office was to be reassured that he would not abandon me and would let me in.

J often encouraged me to speak up about my early childhood relationship with my mother. I found that hard. My experience of her seemed to be missing from inside me. He would ask if it was difficult for me to go to bed as a young child. I mostly had no reply.

But after Peter ended the relationship, a profound sense of abandonment hung over the couch. The hours to the next session stretched ahead, a grey slate of despair. Then J offered me an extra individual meeting. It was generous of him, because I had gathered that he no longer worked in town on certain days. So, when he next swung open his door, I thought, *God, could he possibly have come in for me?*

Because, after years of interminable three-piece suits, the man was wearing a polo neck! A truly dreadful polo neck.

One of the group members was giving out hell. At the end of the evening, J commented that real love was holding someone when they are kicking and screaming, knowing deep down that they want to be held. He often reminded me of this in individual sessions.

'Trust that the same care will be on offer to you.'

The group was teaching me about being human. I was coming to see myself through the mirror of others, to recognise how easy it was to reject the possibilities of self-soothing in favour of self-suffering. A good night in the group revived the insight I had grasped after Carmel's death: that differences of opinion or background do not really matter. What matters is people. The group taught me to accompany others in the valley of sorrow, to trust that the heart has its own rhythm, that people say what they need to say in a manner and at a time that is unique to them. *Other people exist. Other people are not me.* I saw how delusional and inflated my own grief was. There was not a hierarchy of suffering in life; there was just suffering.

The group also taught me about the pain of missed connections. One evening I tried talking to the group about hiding in the corridor, waiting for the bomb to go off. No one spoke, yet this was not a listening silence.

After a while, J commented that I had shared a very frightening experience. He wondered what might be happening for members in the strained atmosphere and talked about the reactions that intense fear can elicit. Still no one said anything.

The group had ended, and I was alone on the stairs when that old hag Terror hijacked me. I went back and knocked on J's door. When it opened, he seemed thrown to see me.

My words were panicked, 'Can't go home … '

His buzzer went, and I realised, *Oh no, he's expecting another patient.*

J quickly assessed the situation, walked over to his desk, returning with crayons and paper.

'I'll be able to give you thirty minutes in an hour's time. Now I want you to sit in the waiting room and draw out these feelings.'

J had recently rented the room next door as a waiting room. The room was cold, yet all that mattered was that he had seen and responded to my terror, had accepted it as genuine. He had not sent me away to manage unbearable feelings on my own.

It was nearly 10 p.m. when we met again.

'I kept telling you that the bomb's got to be locked away or it shatters everything.' I accused him angrily.

'What if the shattering has already taken place?'

We both looked at the paper, covered with red and black slashes.

J said that the feelings had been assigned to the page now, that there was more to me than these feelings, that they were not all of who I was, even if that was not how it felt inside. He reiterated his assertion that my psyche would not cast up something unless I was ready for it. He said, 'If the group fails you, it is out of their humanness, their fragility. Can you identify the "you" in other people? The child who couldn't speak ... the lost mother who couldn't intervene with father ... the child who keeps going back, looking for the idealised father to take care of her ... and, always, this terror of abandonment.'

I thought J would be angry with me when I walked out of the group again, a few weeks later. However, the mood of the following couch session was empathetic. He talked about the tragedy of depriving myself of a response from others, the flight in the face of what could not be handled, the repeating personal pattern: going at life alone. Then he added that he, too, had once walked out of an analytic group – I could not imagine it – and how he had had to think to himself, 'What's going on here?' and return, even though it had been hard to work it through. I felt honoured that he could entrust me with his personal experience. He knew what it was like.

'You survived the only way you knew how,' J said. 'There is another way, and you are capable of it.'

I told him about a recent dream in which I had seen myself crawling back to sanity. J referred to my attachment to Father, to himself, to the unavailable, not moving beyond the trap of early incestuous feelings. The couch session ended with his usual exhortation: 'Let the group in.'

That evening, I found myself in an unusual position: the only woman in the circle. A recently joined member, Mark, was there. He was the same age as me and I liked him.

I told the men about my dream. Mark turned to me admiringly, 'You've a capacity to feel. You don't shirk from your feelings.' He talked about how he had killed off his. Now the other men were speaking up: how feelings seemed to be like water washing over a stone and how they did not seem to really exist, how they had the sense of going through the motions.

For the first time, I wondered if I could offer something to a man because I knew how to feel. J commented that I was valuable in a group, connecting members to feelings of loss, grief and loneliness.

Then the conversation turned to a subject on which, unfortunately, I could contribute nothing: sex. Mark said in an ordinary, easy-going tone how sex was a messy business. It was the first time that I had ever heard a man talk openly about sex. His low-key warmth conveyed, 'You don't have to know everything. It doesn't have to be perfect. It's how sex is.'

Some of the men agreed that speaking in the group felt more naked than sex. I looked at them blankly: how could anything be more intimate than sex? I thought, *Well, if I can handle the group ...*

That night, I felt less intimidated. The men had reached me with their solidarity. I went home and wrote in my journal, 'Feel comforted. Heard Mother's heartbeat.'

6

Dazzling truth

The Truth must dazzle gradually
Or every man be blind—

Emily Dickinson, 'Poem 1129'

READING THE newspapers you would think the only people in therapy were the trendy intelligentsia of New York's Greenwich Village or the middle classes of London's Primrose Hill. Yet there I was, in battered Belfast, scraping together every penny to go to a room with a couch and a circle. Most of the time was spent attending to the scars of what it was to be human and wounded – in that our conversations were no different to those exchanged in multiple languages across the globe. However, some moments in the process belonged to Northern Ireland, to Sinn Féin, to Ourselves Alone.

Near J's office a bevy of police officers are turning back pedestrians. White police tape trails across a street, like wayward ribbon escaped from a wedding cake. A rogue car sits in splendid isolation.

'Sorry, love. You can't go down there.'

Word is going around the gathering crowd that bomb scares are all over the city. I run down a side street. Another cluster of dark-green uniforms appears. I am getting worried: what if J's building has been evacuated too? There is a third possible route. Bored people are milling outside offices, fags and umbrellas in hand. J's office comes into sight, beyond the clutch of tape, on the right side of freedom.

His turret room is removed from the street chaos below.

'You must have been frightened, yet you still came.'

It is as if J is communicating: *You're allowed to be frightened. Trust me. I can hold you in this.* And, with the accumulated stress of my attempts to get there, combined with the anxiety that I would not make it, the tears flow.

Daddy's mad with fear. 'Get down on the floor.' I'm huddled in giggles, beside my sister. Crack, crack. It sounds like Christmas crackers, only better. It's so silly. Shouts are in the street, people running. I'm not laughing any more. There is a horrible, sick feeling in my tummy.

Daddy is crawling to the door, disappearing into the night street to check what is happening. Daddy, don't leave us. *He won't listen. I can't remember my prayers. I get the lines mixed up, so I have to keep it simple: 'I promise, God, I'll do the washing-up and the drying and the garden and anything you want. Just make Daddy come back to me and make the noise stop.'*

The next morning, it's on the news. A woman shot dead near our house. A gift falls into my cornflakes. The plastic wrapping is hard to open. It's easy to pretend I'm not listening because Mummy has that low whisper on her that means 'This is not for the children.' She's saying, 'Brendan, what are we going to do?'

There was a chaotic feeling in the group, with helicopters prowling outside and several members arriving late because of police checkpoints. Someone had heard a news bulletin about suspected trouble. J mentioned in the opening minutes something about what did members need to do in order to be fully present?

As the group got started, I silently fretted: *What if the area is being cleared without us knowing? What if a bomb goes off, and showers of glass fall on top of me because I'm sitting near the window?*

'J, can I use your phone to ring the police?'

I had cut right across the flow of the group. J did not respond. He kept that infuriating analytical impassiveness going, as if he might deign to reply to me in an hour's time, when he had thought through the precise psychological meaning of my question. Or maybe he was challenging me: 'What are you going to do if I don't give you the authority you are investing in me?'

I thought, *he doesn't know what can happen when people forget you.*

It was that time before mobile phones. What should I have done? Bloody well stood up and defiantly used his phone, potentially antagonising him more? Or sat on, the capacity to act freezing over? Or got up and said, 'I don't feel safe here,' and, if the others had refused to leave, left anyway?

But if the bomb had gone off, I could not have lived with myself. I would have betrayed them. So, at least if we stayed together, we would die together.

All this was taking place in my mind within seconds.

Suddenly rage infused me, and the odd thought, *I can't let myself die like this again.*

'Right. I'll ring from the street.'

Before there could be any reaction, I had slung on my coat and was tripping down the stairs, once more defying group etiquette.

An army patrol car was in the street.

'Yes, there's a suspect bomb,' the soldier told me.

'We're up there,' I said, pointing to J's office.

'Well, you're on the boundary of the cleared area. It's up to you whether you stay or leave.'

When I returned to the group, I passed on the soldier's information. We decided to stay. It was the North; the task of assessing probabilities was constant. But J continually looked for opportunities to develop dialogue about the ubiquitous violence in Northern Ireland, while we, random representatives of the population, ignored it, pretending that we were living in Birmingham and that what was going on – shooting, bombing and beatings – was normal, which it had almost become by 1991.

J possessed a moral fury that had not gone underground. However, his was an arduous task because it was dangerous to open up politics in a society where you had to be careful about self-revelation, where the skill of protecting yourself by interpreting linguistic and cultural codes had been ingrained from childhood.

He was developing some of his thought-provoking themes, about what happened when the dialogue stopped and the killing took over, and the immaturity of some of our local politicians who had let us down. What were we unconsciously letting the terrorists carry for us and could we take that projection back and deal with it, learn to think and talk in a society where thinking and talking were floundering, with horrific consequences?

On a bad day I would get caught up in my internal spider's web and hear that I was being personally blamed for the entire history of the Troubles, that it was *all my fault* that taxi drivers were being taken up alleyways and murdered. I would also get annoyed, hearing that it was primarily psychotherapists (or him) who were committed to change, whereas I knew many people in my own creative community working hard for peace.

Yet it was the first time I had ever heard anyone putting forward a cohesive premise for the craziness abounding, which, surely, could not be explained solely in political terms. J was commenting on the unconscious dynamics linked to power in Northern Ireland, wondering if what was taking place in the group might relate to this. What he was implying was that the members looked to him, as the seat of authority, to sort things out, without themselves taking on individual responsibility. While there might have been a fundamental truth in his proposition, I felt enraged and denied.

'I *was* taking on responsibility. You wouldn't even answer me when I asked if I could use your phone.'

It was turning into one of those nights when I would experience J as the most insufferably smug and condescending of gits. He started pontificating that in circumstances of fear and confusion politeness was no longer required.

'So I was expected to change my behaviour, but yours remained the same?' I argued. If he represented government, he had the hypocrisy of the British government, the way there was no such thing as proper voting – *getting angrier* – there was no real democracy, it was all a pretence. Reaching down into fury, I hurled at him, 'I feel completely disenfranchised.'

J replied, so superciliously removed from the emotional fray that I hated him for it, 'That's why you're in therapy.'

I heard him telling me that I did not have a right to feel what I felt, that my feelings were the product of my screwed-up world which he was dismissing from on high.

'Don't you ever fucking do that again!' I shouted at him.

It was unheard of for me to curse in the outside world, yet I was letting myself experience what rage felt like in a body that felt alive. He was murmuring something about a family story around disenfranchisement – I could not hear him – something about anger potentially being a transformational life force. He was acknowledging that I was, indeed, the only member who had acted.

The following morning it was the lead story on the news: one of the largest car bombs ever found in Northern Ireland, defused near J's office. We had got away with it again.

For many months I walked down that long, stony road in therapy, making conscious connections with my own family story, letting myself say the un-sayable and feeling my own anger and frustration. But looking back on that night in the group, as I write now, what strikes me most is how much I wanted to live.

> Dream, September 1991
> The individual session is taking place at night-time, in my childhood bedroom, the one opposite the police station. I'm standing alone by the window, crying, my head buried in my hands. J calls me over to him and puts his hand on mine. The dream has a numinous quality of comfort, the sense that J understands me and knows what I need.
> Then I realise that I am naked, but it's OK, it's not sexual. J is telling me what to do with the sharp objects, yet his words are so dense that I can hardly take them in. The dream then changes. I am going into the group, feeling shaken, but the circle is full of unrecognisable people.

For days I have been wondering could I reveal my most vulnerable 'naked' self to J. I have also been reflecting on recent changes. My Monday morning individual session has been moved to early Monday evening, in order to accommodate J's teaching schedule for a term. That means I have only a ten-minute break between the individual session and the group. I feel torn going immediately from one to the other.

On the couch, I tell J about my dream and speak about the knot inside me, how I want to open up about difficulties in my past. J misses my cue.

'It is not that easy because the past is not separate from the present. It continues to be enacted in the here and now. It's not that you used to hurt yourself physically, but continue to do so emotionally. You cause difficulties for yourself, place yourself in situations where you get hurt. You turn anger against yourself. You box yourself in with sharp ideas, with self-critical concepts, in how you think.' He goes on: 'A lot of splitting is going on in the therapy. I have become the idealised, all-good one and the group is the cruel, sadistic one. You want complete beneficence from me, the perfect feed. You want to hold on to a special relationship with me, to get my total attention. You don't want to share me. You seek out differences in order to diminish the others, so that only I exist. This is about early infant attachment with Mother, the longing to be in the womb again, how hard it is to let go.'

If only I could grasp these giant concepts, fuzzily beyond my reach. If only I did not feel.

'I'm lost,' I concede.

In demoralised moments like these, I feel invariably pulled towards defeat, worn out by the interminable challenge of therapy.

J responds, 'That is a hard place to be.'

There is a tense silence between us. I find myself thinking about knots: the sick knot inside me, the impossible knot in my relationship with J, the memory of a fisherman's net, lying knotted on a chipped blue and yellow boat. My mind wanders off, trying to unravel dilemmas with my inadequate intellect. The task is beyond me. I do not speak for a long time. There is no way out. I will forever be trapped.

Then something quite uncanny happens. J murmurs, 'Knots can be important.'

Have I magically transferred the image in my mind to him because I have not spoken about knots since the first opening minutes?

J stirs again. 'Isn't it the knots that give wood its character?'

He has taken the session in the wrong direction (he should have gone with my willingness to open up about the past). Yet we can still share a creative, symbolic language that allows a knotted feeling to become a fisherman's net, to become a piece of bark.

Hope stirs.

After months of reading *The Independent*, I decided that I did not, after all, want J to be my shadow. I felt stronger inside.

The Guardian and I had an elated reunion in the expensive café, reserved for treat cappuccinos after brilliant sessions. (The backstreet caff with bog-brown tea and fried chips was for the miserable ones.) There had to be another way for two people to work together, one that allowed us both to be individual and different.

It is September 1991 when two themes collide in a Monday couch session. The first is about being special; the second about being in search of the truth. 'What if I can't handle the truth?' I had asked J. He had replied, 'We can deal with the truth in here. My role is to help.'

Now J adopts a fierce, dogmatic tone. He is going to set me straight about an illusion I have been indulging in.

'You – are – not – special.'

Serrated knife tears through wafer-thin skin with appalling accuracy. He has found the black hole in me.

The individual session must have ended. Mouths are moving, voices speaking. I must be in the group. Not enough time to hide. A member is addressing a question to me. Consonants are reeling, clumping, whirling.

'J says ...' – *Father, Mother, J* – 'I'm not ...' – *never have been, never will be* – 'special.' *The truth, the whole truth and nothing but the truth, so help me God.*

In eighteen months, I have never seen anyone cry in the group; now the room reverberates with the sobbing of a wounded animal. I think the sounds are coming from me. Damien launches into a ramble. J interrupts him. 'Can you bear to be with her crying?'

So I am to be allowed to cry. The group looks on, stunned. Eventually Anna breaks the spell. 'Why do you take what J says so much to heart? I used to do that but, now, I've more of a sense of my own judgement.'

There are more words. I cannot take them in. The group must be ending. J is moving over to his office desk. The others are hovering, not sure what to do. I studiously pack and unpack my handbag, avoiding any eye contact, telling myself harshly to pull myself together. My weeping will not cease.

There are the stairs to negotiate. When I had first started combined therapy, J had so emphasised his 'no contact' rule that I had dreaded the thought of going down the stairs afterwards, afraid of inadvertently breaking boundaries. The others had initiated me into the way of it: a light phrase or two, a smile if things had gone well, a yielding silence if badly, no reference to the substance of the night, just enough to carry us down to the front door, where we would disappear into the fabric of our own lives.

The others are ahead of me, slowing down at every turn in the stairwell so that I can catch up. I am holding back from the communal flow, my oldest unconscious survival strategy in times of distress. Soon I will be at the front door and they will have gone on. No. They are waiting for me. There are subdued 'goodnight's because this is the group, this is what we have to do, but tonight is different. Someone is stepping in. Someone is saying, 'I'll drive you home.'

It is Tom. Tom who suffers and is in pain. Tom, my enemy.

We are not supposed to meet outside, but what does anything matter now? Nothing is exchanged in the short car journey except for my tearful directions. If we do not have a proper conversation, we can pretend to ourselves that we are not breaking the group rules, which we know we are. Nearing my flat, a thought enters my head: *can't go home*. I ask Tom would he mind taking me to a friend's house. We drive there. The car stops.

Tom turns to me, 'Are you sure you'll be all right? What if your friend's not in? I'll wait. If she's not there, I'll take you wherever you want to go.'

In the car, under the autumnal streetlight, I look up, and, for the first time, I see Tom. I see his decency, his capacity for love and kindness. Yet, going up the path, I know that what has happened has taken place outside the group where it belongs.

The following Monday evening, members directed a barrage of concerned questions to me. J intervened early. 'I'm sure she can hear the group's compassion for her. It might help her more if we could think about that part in each of us yearning to be special. Could we talk about what she might be holding for the whole group, take back what belongs to each of us, so that she doesn't have to carry it all?'

There would be no more pitching in from me, no more responding to J's invitation to speak out thoughts and feelings (which only got me into trouble), no more being *good*. It was not that this most special person in my world had stated an implacable, existential truth: 'You are not special' – a terrible thought in itself. No, I had heard J conveying a specific message so that I would back away from him with my cloying intensity. 'You're not special *to me*. You never have been and you never will be. *No one* has a special place in their heart for you.'

Letter extract, 7 October 1991

I have found these past few weeks harrowing. It is as if my life has been lit up with a dazzling light. All my life I yearned to be special, to be loved. How do you convey what it is like to know that you are not the special one? It sounds easy to accept, and it is not. To be not special was not to be able to exist, to be annihilated.

The dark feeling when you told me I was not special ... What you said devastated me and sent me out into the wilderness. It was a shattering experience. I felt you brutally rejected me – the love and respect I had offered, the effort and discipline I had invested in therapy. I felt wounded to the core, like the old wounds were reopened to salty air.

I have thought a lot about what you said: about thinking of myself as 'different', 'individual', 'unique' – rather than 'special'. How to come to terms with the sadness that I am not special to you, to Father or Mother, and yet, somehow, I still have value.

You never led me to believe that I was special, J, so it should not have shocked me. It did. You are a good therapist. You said what you said for therapeutic reasons, but it has been hard. I have been face to face with the damaged, suicidal me. I've been frightened and still am.

In this Gethsemane hour, my sister stepped back into my life; we really did not know each other. Yet, through combined therapy, I had become aware that I was constantly configuring a shadowy figure wherever I went: the woman who was more pretty/popular/clever than me, whom Father/Mother/authority publicly praised, whereas I was the one who was more difficult to love.

I realised that I could not blame my sister for how I felt about myself. That was my responsibility. I was not being fair on her. I felt guilty for having shut her out, and, underneath everything, I discovered that I loved her.

In November 1991, I met my sister in London and found myself confiding in her about being in therapy. I just said it, 'I felt you were the special one.' It was the first time that I had ever talked about the dynamic that had dominated my relationship with her. From there, we went on to talk about the past. Until then my greatest hope had been that I had been lying to J, that there had never been any bombs. Now I knew that what I had been saying was true.

'Do not talk outside about what it is going on in therapy.' J's couch advice was helpful. An old self was dying, and a new self needed healing silence in order to reform. The group helped me to endure depression.

'I've been thinking about you.'

'How've you been?'

'I've been worried about you.'

Members talked about what the longing to be special meant to them. I listened and heard through their sharing that I was not even special in wanting to be special, yet that felt like a consolation rather than a further attack. They were looking after me in a broken place.

Damien seemed particularly upset for me. He said the theme of 'special' meant a lot to him, that he was gaining from me, and vice versa. He passed me the box of tissues when I was crying, a small gesture, but I was learning that small gestures make a difference. 'Can't ordinary people be special?' he mused. 'Isn't there a special-ness in the ordinary?'

I kept faith by turning up, even though I often did not speak. A thought was forming inside: *Could there be a release in accepting that I was limited and ordinary? Would it mean that I would not have to keep on exhaustingly striving?* Because a part of me could never feel special enough, no matter whatever magnificent gesture the external world made. According to

J, this was about an *internal* deficit, some early experience of not feeling seen and loved at a deep level of self, about coming into contact with an idealised self and grieving.

After four months of depression, light began to glimmer again in the no-hope tunnel. I felt a rising desire to get actively involved in group life, to give back to the members who had given so much to me. I had no idea of the catastrophic couch interpretation that J was about to make.

'You have changed. There has been a death and a rebirth. You have made room for other people. You are in the final stages of therapy and will leave soon.'

The hidden power structure in therapy had been revealed: it was J who owned and controlled the process. When I found my couch voice, it was upset. 'Couldn't you have trusted me enough to let me direct you?'

Worse still was the realisation that I had become the most dreaded of clichés: the patient who had fallen in love with her therapist. J had been perfectly willing to let me go. I represented nothing to him beyond a clinician's duty of care, at which he excelled. But I now knew that I loved him and could not bear to leave him.

How on earth could I love him when I knew little about him? After each summer break, I would ask, 'Did you have a nice time?'

J would reply, 'Excellent, thank you.'

That would be it. If I pressed for more, he would be strict: 'You're not paying me to talk about me.' Eventually I gave up.

Yet love – no other word could describe it – was what I felt when I connected to the soul qualities that flowed through him: calmness, clarity, compassion, strength and gentleness. So this was the poisoned chalice of therapy: coming to depend on someone, opening my heart, and for it all to be one-sided.

In the early hours of the morning I lay awake, wondering if this pitch of panic could indeed be a re-enactment of early separation, as J had suggested, some replaying of early shock, fright or loss. I was also reflecting on J's tough comments: how I always had to have some high-octane drama to be caught up in, this pattern of ricocheting from one crisis to another. He warned me that if I was not careful, I could end up like the boy in Aesop's fable, *The Boy Who Cried Wolf*, crying alarm so regularly that when a real wolf came, the villagers did not believe him. It was painful to hear. It was true.

At 4 a.m. I switched on the light and wrote a letter to J. I told him that my new self was too fragile and unsure to be faced with separation. I asked him to trust me. And as I wrote, I remembered J's words: 'I am not rejecting you. I am here for you, for as long as you need me.'

As it turned out, I needed him for another four years.

Raking the soil of one internal layer leads to the earth beneath it becoming unsettled. This is how a psychoanalytic therapy can shift organically into deeper strata, with the older, buried seeds becoming dislodged.

A long forgotten experience skips onto the couch.

Seven or eight years old. Being left off at my new primary school when an idea forms in my head. I'm going to play a secret game. The game's called 'No One's Going to See Me Unhappy'. I turn around with a smile – you see, just like that, the game has begun – and kiss Mummy and Daddy goodbye. I'm walking up the path thinking, Remember, the game's not over until you go to bed. If anyone sees you sad, you've lost. *I was clever. I won. The next day I played it again. I became the best in the world at my game.*

One day I hear my aunt laughing. I think, I'll never lose if I'm always laughing. *Now I am practising my aunt's laugh. My natural giggle is fading, disappearing beneath a fixed portrait painting. I can't remember the sound of my own child's laugh. I've sold it, for an adult's, for the sake of my game.*

J listens intently, and then he responds with heartfelt compassion, 'I feel so sad for the child who could not be who she was.'

And, just like that, a tsunami of grief and awareness surges in.

Letter extract, 17 May 1992
I don't know who I am, and that is such a frightening feeling.

I found Thursday's session helpful. I had a sense of the trapped, panic-stricken, terrified parts of myself, sealed away in a cupboard or a coffin. It helped me make sense of the loneliness that has been bothering me. I feel so lonely. It doesn't relate to external things; it's a hollowness deep within. Somehow, in therapy, I can be lonely with you, and with the group, and feel what that is like. It makes me unbelievably sad. I feel full of haunting sorrow, for what or whom, I do not know.

7
The black pit

Unless both doctor and patient become a problem to each other, no solution is found.

Carl Jung, *Memories, Dreams, Reflections* (1963)

WE ARE locked in a vicious war. J is not of this mortal world. He is a thundering Goliath, gratingly admonishing 'analyse, analyse,' targeting my personality with his elite, winged army of interpretations. Vengeance has to be planned carefully, seeking out the weakness that a patient can find. He will be made to retreat from his ruthless pursuit of the truth. I have one nasty stone in my makeshift catapult; sometimes one is all you need, if you choose your moment.

'What do you know about grief?' I comment nastily. 'You've never grieved in your life.'

The Bad Giant is swaying, a victory for the victimised David. I have set out to hurt him, as I have felt hurt by him. At the parting door I see a flicker in his eyes and feel shame.

I write shopping lists of J's depressing feedback about me:

- unhealthy passions
- inability to handle ambivalence
- oscillating between polarities of idealisation and despair
- desperate for affirmation, yet hearing negation
- yearning for love, yet having difficulties taking love in.

Now he knows me too well, is consumed with the kinks that give him an opportunity to dazzle as a therapist. He wants to unpick my crooked fabric and to re-knit me. I cannot breathe, entrapped in his version of me, and a patient-self is embedding itself in response.

'You won't allow me to change,' I tell him, frustrated.

Our work lists and lolls, stuck in the doldrums. He says he sees what is happening in the room, but does not explain what he means. Then I remember a long-forgotten exchange from my first year on the couch, when I admitted that I did not understand what everything meant, and J replied – a glorious moment – that neither did he.

Peter is back. Actually, he has never really left. Weeks after our romance had ended, I had written to Peter, wanting to take responsibility for what I, too, might have contributed to the break-up. We had met and agreed to go on as friends. Now, in September 1992, nearly four years into therapy, we have decided to try again as partners.

The first person to be informed of the joyous news is, of course, J, but J seems disapproving, his prodding questions impossible to answer. How do I know if Peter is freed from the past and understands what happened last time? I find myself silently speculating: what if the situation was reversed and Peter was J's patient? Would J give me a chance or hint that Peter might be better off with someone with fewer difficulties?

The room resonates with J's strong sense of professional responsibility. 'I care for you. You are in *my* care.'

How I have longed to hear these words, only not in this context. J sees a possible pattern with Peter and urges caution. I want to go my own sweet way. He is like Mummy and Daddy. Everyone is allowed a boy, except me. No one is good enough.

I wail, 'Aren't you always saying that people nowadays aren't willing to work at relationships, that embracing risk is important?'

I know: Love will out.

I thought I was attempting in the group what J had repeatedly invited – moving out towards other. J's after comment, therefore, felt all the more horrifying: 'The virgin maiden who bleeds.'

He was using an obvious word, a painful word, one I had never owned for myself in the group. I felt humiliatingly labelled. Then I did what I always did: I walked out.

Five minutes before the group ended – when there was no time to responsibly resolve anything – I came back in. After the meeting was over, I marched up to J's desk and heard J's frustration with me too.

'Why do you think I would spend energy putting you down? I'm angry with you because of what you don't tell the group.'

So we are, once more, caught in a tangle. Because he cannot remember how hard it is to talk about private, painful matters, he forgets that I am trying. He cannot trust me. And I cannot hold on to the good. I cannot remember that he cares. I cannot trust him. Dispiritingly, round and round we go.

I was working on the children's festival on a full-time basis by now; I had fallen in love with it. I could not admit that the project was overextended and under-resourced. J advised, 'Maturity means defining your limits.'

Everything ran into trouble in the autumn of 1992. A key member of staff became unavailable, highlighting that the programme of events was too ambitious. I had also foolishly agreed to serve on a film jury abroad. I rang J from Germany, crying. He said, 'Ring me tomorrow at 3.40 p.m.'

The next day it was such a security to hear his steady voice, to let it come out how I seemed driven to inflict punishing pressure on myself, how I could not allow myself the pleasure that I wanted for children. What had I done to deserve this level of punishment? J suggested that I write down my associations with 'pressure', both internal and external, to tide me over until we met again.

For the rest of that winter, we worked on the theme of me taking better care of myself. But that day, that day on the phone in Germany, all that mattered was that he was there for me.

The insomnia triggered by Carmel's murder, and combined with therapy's impact on my psyche, never lifted. One day, at the end of a couch session, J picked up the amethyst crystal on the small table beside his chair.

'Maybe this will help.'

From then on I went to bed clutching his crystal.

With Peter, I discovered anew that I was not asexual, that, amazingly, I loved to kiss and be kissed, to touch and be touched. Sexual intercourse was an area of fear, so Peter and I did not go there, but we explored the possibility of sensual pleasure. Mostly I enjoyed our cups of coffee, his smile and our conversations. Peter had the gift of containing my anxiety, yet I did not seem to have the same facility with him.

A few months into our renewed relationship, something was troubling Peter, and I feared that our romance might be over again. Somehow or other we went on. Inside I worried: was the bond between us based on an unconscious recognition of shared sadness? Were we wrong for each other, even though we were fond of each other?

On the couch, I kept wheedling J. 'You don't believe my relationship with Peter is going to work, do you?'

Finally, he cracked: 'If you must have an answer … no.'

Afterwards, J commented tersely that I had lured him into a trap; mostly he seemed annoyed with himself for falling into it. Now there were two cross people in the room, both of whom felt in a no-win situation.

Letter extract, 4 June 1993
You'll deny this: I think you're totally fed up with me. The work has lost its creativity. We are trudging on, bickering, rowing, both refusing to accept the other's point of view. You're as guilty as I am. I don't know what the dissolution of a marriage is like – no doubt a telling comment – I imagine it's like this, trying to make something work that's gone.

What once seemed a comforting bond now seems a bind. I feel dragged along some way that doesn't seem my way. If I make any comments you snap at me; equally I snap your head off. We're encumbered with each other, sick of each other, and stuck with each other. I've got to the point where I think we hate each other. You won't acknowledge this. You keep pretending everything's all right, yet you can't handle what I say.

I don't care any more if I never get to the top of Everest. I'm exhausted from the climb. You retort, well, you can leave any time, but it would be tragic to know that my attempt had failed, given my fascination with the mountain. That would stay with me for the rest of my life. It's not an easy question of giving up, of saying to hell with it. I wish I could. It was a serious commitment.

Yes, we've had arguments and rows; they flared up, and we moved on. Now we're in a quagmire, a bog of resentment and friction. Nothing's growing there. Everything's dead or dying, fossilised, squelching, muddy.

One day, light broke through on the couch. I saw for myself how I had turned away from intimacy out of woundedness. I connected to my own desire to go beyond history, to stop unconsciously recycling the past, to choose for myself what I wanted. I did not want to keep on denying myself sexuality. I wanted to be a loving, passionate woman, to claim that as my enjoyable birthright.

However, I needed to know that Peter was committed to the relationship. Peter said yes. We agreed that I would go on the pill, a huge signifier in itself. We would travel to Italy, my first holiday with a lover. Against a backdrop of sunny relaxation, we would commit to a greater level of love and trust.

Letter extract, July 1993
My dear J,

A long time ago I made a promise to myself to write about the phases and colours of therapy. I want to honour that and to tell you how much I have loved and have been loved at your office. I have loved you. It may have been an unreal fantasy, a secret world of imaginary friends and lovers, but it has also been a marvellous freedom, the freedom to hope that I could love a man and that a man could be caring to me. I have let myself feel what it is like to reveal oneself to a man, to hurt and be hurt, to trust and be trusted, to pretend that I could have a lover, be a lover.

Often I wrote about what I wanted to express for you, yet rarely could I let myself feel love from you. Yet since Peter and I have found each other, I see how you have shown me such real love and thought. It wasn't just your consistency, the fact that you never complained about my phone calls, letters, my demands, my coming back after sessions. It was your belief in my ability to love, your encouragement to experience myself as a woman. It was also something else – I can't put it into words – your ability to connect to my spirit, the thoughts that could not be expressed, my desires long shut away.

Before therapy, I remember doing a meditation where I visualised my sexuality as an empty bowl, dry, covered in dust, unused. I feel you've been with me as I touched that bowl. In my mind's eye you've put your arms around me and held me as I have cried away sorrow. Yet underneath – and no one could have seen it – I think the bowl was beautiful. I can't get over the colour in there, in me. You believed in those colours.

We've had some terrible times. I'm sure I've wounded you with my criticisms, harshness and anger. I acknowledge, not too late I hope, your loving spirit. I'm not leaving therapy – I couldn't yet. I am saying goodbye to J – the lover, enemy, father, teacher, whom I could love with all my heart, safe in the knowledge that we would never be sexual. I want to let the fantasies go. They served a very creative, valuable purpose. They gave me a dream world that gave me hope. If I had the courage to fantasise that you were my surrogate partner, then it must have meant I was capable of being and having a lover. That helped my confidence as a woman. Yet I want to move into the reality of the world.

I have needed you, J, to guide me in my darkest forest. We have travelled many woods together and befriended many wolves. Peter is with me now. He and I must be on our own to see how we cope. I must trust Peter and myself. A leave-taking is taking place. A part of me doesn't want to let you go, yet I feel full of connection to you and you are lovingly wishing me on. I am honoured and grateful.

J's office was closed for August when the inner crisis erupted for Peter, a fortnight before we were due to go away. It was then that my heart told me: this relationship cannot give me the security that I need. The flights could not be refunded, so the options were to stay in Belfast or to travel abroad as friends. I had to make the best decision that I could, without J.

Peter and I went to Italy. I think I was still hoping that the dream would come right. It was a disastrous decision. For two days and two nights Peter and I shredded everything that had been good between us. Then it was somehow agreed that Peter would leave; he had someone to go to. I stayed on. For hours I sat at the café where Peter and I had drunk cappuccinos. It was irrational, but I believed that he would come back. And, finally, the hour came when I knew that I was alone, that the relationship with Peter had ended, and ended terribly.

'I'm going to break the rules because I want to respond to you. I'm not neutral. I'm angry.'

There was a time when J would never have said this. Something is changing in him, a willingness to respond more humanly, a greater synthesising of psychoanalytic and psychosynthetic approaches, so that the two flow more in harmony. The analytic rules mean a lot to him; out of respect for them, he rarely gives a personal opinion. To break the rules, it had to have been important.

'I think you handled this situation with dignity. If this had happened to one of my daughters, I would want a man to say to her what I'm saying to you.'

'Daughter' has come in again and, with her, the usual upsurge of paternal tenderness. It feels as if I am included in a circle of love, by subliminal association. It feels good to evoke the protection of Father. Father is whom I ache for in a crisis. I feel safe being an eternal child-daughter. I tell J that I will never try again for a relationship with a man.

'I'm sad to hear that. I know this has been a dreadful experience. What about bringing the learning to your next relationship, shaping new choices? Think of the progress you've experienced. You can have another relationship, and it can be better.'

'I can't believe anyone would ever love me.'

'Do you really love yourself?'

J's question seems simple, yet its challenge is far-reaching.

'Find yourself an ordinary man, just an ordinary man with strengths and weaknesses. Leave the broken-hearted people to me.'

I told the group about what had happened in Italy. Apparently, I said that there had been blood and shattered glass everywhere, even though there was no reality to this. A new member, a woman my own age, Eva, got out of her chair and hugged me.

I was quiet on the couch. I spent my time watching the weak sunrays dancing on the carpet, although light was limited these days. The ever-present lump in my throat meant that I could not rally the energy to talk, and, anyway, I had nothing meaningful to offer.

One day, in low, rolling cadences, J spoke about the natural laws that govern the seasons, how the fields could give the appearance of fallowness, yet the seeds were sheltering underground. Winter was a period of hibernation and incubation, when energy could restore itself. There could be a spiritual intelligence in staying low to the ground, but the ground itself was not dead. Green spring always came back. J's haiku images were like fronds coiling around a damaged soul. Hope was being planted and watered at the right time, in a spirit of loving kindness.

Another day when I was on the couch, J related a myth about some goddess who had been grievously hurt and who gathered her nymphs around her for support.

'Couldn't you do that with your female friends, and the women in the group, hmmm? Wouldn't that help rally you?'

I was very touched because the man, as he said himself, was not a feminist, was not any sort of '-ist'.

The days went by.

The weeks went by.

The months went by.

I did not write to J any more.

Northern Ireland continued plunging into violent mayhem, with twenty-three people murdered in one week. In the couch silence, J murmured something unusual: 'The Northern Irish psyche is changing.'

He sounded so sure that I had to hope he could see something with his unique eagle-eye perspective which I could not.

Independent international cinema was not J's first cultural love, but I think he went to see Jane Campion's *The Piano* for me in the autumn of 1993. I was, again, touched. He was willing to come down into my modernist world and give it a chance. Still, we could only agree on two aspects of the film: that it was brilliantly directed and brilliantly acted. Thereafter, our opinions diverged.

J argued (trenchantly and at considerable length) that the leading female character, Ada (played by Holly Hunter), was a talented yet wilfully stubborn and spoiling woman, hurting the people around her when other choices were possible. I loved her.

For months, even years, we explored a rich tapestry of psychological and spiritual themes through the medium of one film. I would talk about my fascination with the brooding Ada, the woman initially unable to speak or love, yet she had an enduring passion for her piano.

Into J's room would swirl eroticism – the scene where Baines (played by Harvey Keitel) stroked the hole in Ada's stocking. *The Piano* gave us a vocabulary to talk about sex. J said, 'Sex is a medium, a threshold for the soul.'

I had long struggled to understand sexuality, never mind the correlation between sexuality and spirituality.

'Sex with someone you love, well, there's nothing else like it,' he said.

The room permeated with wonder, a man standing up sensually for a template of loving sex.

'There will be men interested in fucking you. That's not you.' J could use pretty robust language sometimes, and, yes, he knows me. 'You say you're a feminist, yet you're traditional in your thinking. You want a man to teach you about the sexual.' I had never thought of it like that. He was right. 'What about taking responsibility for your own pleasure, getting to know your own orgasm?' I was shocked. He was treating me like an adult sexual woman, not a girl-princess, locked away in a fairy castle. I did not know how to tell him that I was afraid of orgasm, that pleasure was confusingly linked in my mind to feelings of depression, that pleasure seemed a lie and pain the truth.

Instead, I talked to J about the ending of *The Piano*. 'You see, Ada deliberately puts her foot into the rope when she asks for her piano to be thrown into the sea. She's drowning,' – I wave the screenplay in my hand – 'and then she fights and emerges with those incredible words, "What a death! What a chance! What a surprise! My will has chosen life!"'

That weekend, I was once again at Eckhart House. (I had been accepted onto their foundation course and was now in Dublin one weekend a month.) Following a guided meditation, I drew myself as Ada, sinking into a watery grave, my foot entangled in chains. Beside the ensnared Ada, I drew a second figure rising from the water with the words, 'Emerge! Life and the Sensual'. As I studied the second woman, I saw that there was something ethereal and romanticised about her, as if she represented the idealised female sexuality that I longed for but could never quite embody. I wrote down an insight: 'I've a deep desire to be sexually alive which I'm also attacking.'

At the same time, reverberating through my mind was the memory of J's undeviating questions in the last couch session: 'Are you willing to disidentify from the attacking part of you? Are you going to take your foot out of the rope? Will you choose life?'

In January 1994, after five years in therapy, J asked what I wanted for myself for the year ahead. I had spent Christmas and the New Year in bed with the flu. A sound-image crystallised over the couch: the chimes playing with the wind in Eckhart House's garden.

'I'd love lightness.'

J endorsed the notion. This was the same man who often groaned 'Lighten up.'

We were enjoying one of those warm-hearted, close conversations that I wanted to go on for ever. He was talking about how, as he grew older (how nice to know he had once been young because he did not seem quite of this world), he had come to value 'nothingness' and dreaming. Intimacy percolated the texture between us: he trusted me enough to bring himself in.

As the conversation developed, I could hear his protective worry for me and wanted to tell him, 'It's OK, you can give up.' He had other patients who would resolve seemingly irresolvable problems; they would be the ones he would remember fondly and write about glowingly in professional journals. He had a highly successful practice. He did not need me to prove the value of therapy, which, for some reason, I had taken onto myself as a task, wanting to get well for him more than for me. He could be allowed a discreet pile of failures.

After five years of faith and hard work, I had not been rewarded with a loving sexual relationship; rather, I had experienced the kind of heartbreak that would never have happened if I had not ventured out in the first place. I did not know anyone else who had been in therapy for as long as me. Time and money were running out. Perhaps J, too, was secretly disappointed, which was why he seemed cross at my inability to move on. It was best that I made the gesture to go.

'You are a wayfarer on a journey. It's not about turning back but following it through to the end. Are you ready to leave?'

I gave a truthful answer. 'No, but I feel I should be.'

'That's different.'

I told him I had been offered a new opportunity: the voluntary chairmanship of an international film association, which would involve a lot of travel. My ego was seduced.

J posed a good question. 'How would that contribute to lightness?'

The more we mulled, the more I knew I had to resist the pull to perpetual motion which only reinforced my inner loneliness. My body needed to rest, to recover and to open up to a concept of fun. So it was that I began to wonder how could I realistically incorporate lightness into my life rather than making 'lightness' a new tyranny. I reflected on J's question: 'What about *being*, not doing?'

Dream, January 1994
I am lying at the far end of the couch, resting my head on J's leg. He is trying hard to talk to me about the concept of self-absorption in a way that I can understand. He has drawn a portrait of me, is quoting poems and moving around the room.
'Have you grasped it?'
'Yes.'
I snuggle up in his arms, feeling loved and tightly held. The dream is imbued with a quality of lightness.
It is time to leave the session. J has transformed into a woman called Dawn. As I am going down the stairs, I realise that I need his portrait of me and turn back. Where is it? Did we throw it out when we were tidying up? No, there it is, bundled with messages of hope. It is then I see that J's painting is of me taking off my mask and revealing my real face. There is a sadness there, and also a letting in of love.

Tom has left the group. I kept thinking, *he can't leave, not without experiencing the promised land of redemption.* I could not find any maturity within myself to help stop the self-destructive pattern unravelling around me, could not persuade Tom out of the corner he felt backed into or had backed himself into. I projected responsibility onto J, thought, *Do something, man. It can't end like this.*

It did.

I had started giving those leaving the group a poem or a gift. It was not the norm, more an idiosyncratic personal gesture. I did not know what to do about Tom. I could not trump up some fake sugary farewell, so I wrote him a card to say how sorry I was for my part in our relationship and to wish him well on his journey. (Although I crossed out the last three words because I knew the word 'journey' would annoy him.) Maybe it was easier to give a card than to talk.

On his last night, Tom made a caustic snipe at me (as I had done a thousand times and more with him). I thought, *what's the point in giving him the card?* However, when he was making his goodbyes, I saw the tight, clenched look on his face and relented.

The following Monday evening, J handed me an envelope. It was a card from Tom in which he wrote how sorry he, too, was for how it had been between us, how he thought I had never seen him, except for that one night when he had driven me home. The card was imbued with the pathos of what could have been and what did not come to pass: the possible and the impossible.

Not everything worked out in therapy. It was real life. There were failures, breakdowns, sadnesses and tragedies. I did not see Tom again, so never knew what happened to him. But I dreamt about him for years.

Two new members joined the group on the same night. I was grateful that this demanding experience had not befallen me; however, Carol and Jeff were therapists, and, in my idealising world, therapists lived on the sunny side of the river. They had the fabulous excuse of telling themselves that they were *really* in the group to advance their professional training, unlike the rest of us genuine stigmata sufferers. I grew to like them both very much. They taught me that therapists did not necessarily have life any easier.

Carol made a particular impact on me at that time. A single mother in her late thirties, she had a gutsy, spirited quality that I admired. One evening she talked about a book she was reading on the gifts of the menstrual cycle, called *Red Moon*. The next day, I ordered it. I just liked being close to Carol, being interested in what she was interested in. I admired how she was brave and open about female sexuality. She was not weak and passive (like me, like my internalised mother figure). She could stand up for herself. (Would she stand up for me?) I looked to her for what was missing in me.

Another evening, Carol spoke about periods with nonchalant confidence, as if encouraging me to talk. She felt like the sexually grounded, female figure I eternally searched for, the one who could help me with the initiation into womanhood which had never happened. When the same conversation about menstruation continued over two or three meetings, some of the men shifted uncomfortably – 'Look here ...'

Carol didn't seem bothered.

Another time, when I was upset, Carol took off the scarf she was wearing and wrapped it around my shoulders. I slept with it, along with J's crystal.

Against this backdrop, in April 1994, I brought a powerful dream into the group. I felt it belonged to us all.

I am walking up a hill on a sunny morning with Carol. We're having a great time. I'm asking her about the town where she lives. Then we go into a large hall where a dancing group is starting. In this group you've got to have 'contact partners'.

I tell Carol, 'We're in the wrong group.'

She shrugs, 'So?' She is going to get involved anyway, but I shrink back, too shy to join in.

A nice older man appears. Meanwhile, young people are running in and out of the hall. One of them comes up to me and says, 'Six-eight-nine.'

I turn to the man, 'What does that mean? Is it aged six or eight or nine? Or a code?'

Carol, this man and I chat, as if at school. The man says to Carol, 'I've met you before in Greece. We went horse-riding together.'

Now J, a threatening, scary figure, comes over to split us up. Carol goes on talking – she is a good-humoured rebel. I'm so afraid, I keep trying to hide.

The man is reassuring me, 'Don't worry. You're considerate, you won't get into trouble.'

J is giving the instructions. He tells the man, 'You're to sit at the bottom of the big table.' Then he turns to me: 'You're to be the woman at the top.'

Then I realise that a horrible game is unfolding: a test in which I've got to do something as a woman. (Or is it to become a woman, to prove that I'm a woman?) I've got to catch a wild chicken and shut it in a room. The chicken is snapping at my feet. I'm petrified to even touch it.

At that moment, a gun goes off.

Carol says, 'Part of the game is that you've a gun to stun other participants.'

In the dream, I am protesting, 'I've been in bombings and shootings, I can't do this. I'm terrified.' I'm getting distraught.

Carol is saying, 'You've got to go through with it. You're in the group.'

I reply, 'I can't face this. I'll have to leave.'

The boys are lining up, the game about to commence. There is a horrific moment when I feel intensely sick terror spreading throughout my body. Then, suddenly, I see that one of the boy contestants is standing still. The entire group is refusing to play. They are insisting that whatever the task is, there has to be another approach for me. I am immensely relieved. The group is looking after me. I won't have to leave.

Then an extraordinary thing happens. Everyone agrees that I can fulfil the task by releasing pollen from these large flowers that have appeared. The group is stressing that the flowers want to release their pollen. They will grow again: the task is not based on destruction. The sky turns yellow with pollen as I am able to manage the task.

However, there is an ominous note at the end of the dream, the feeling that I have escaped the task this once but will be made to face it another time.

I wake up feeling afraid.

Carol responded first. 'That's obviously about the sexual, isn't it?' She sounded embarrassed for me, and I was disappointed at her reaction. However, I knew that I needed to honour this dream by recalling it exactly as it was, no matter what response it evoked in anyone else. After four years in the group, this magnificent soul dream achieved the impossible: it created a pathway to talk to fellow members about my difficulties with sexuality. The dream had come to help me, but it was not going to 'out' me. It was willing to provide a symbolic canopy under which I could shelter if I got too frightened.

Talking with the group released new insights. I saw how the pull in me towards depression linked to some terrorising, bullying internal part of myself. The others kept telling me, 'You're so hard on yourself.' That night, I wrote in my journal the feelings inspired by the group experience: *safe*, *loved*, *secure*, *warm*, *cared for*, *held*. The dream's message had come true: the group was looking after me.

I also recorded the rare and moving statement that J had publicly addressed to me at the end of the evening: 'I open my heart to you.'

J was summoning up his inner resources to connect with me on the couch. 'If you are sick of suffering, I rejoice.'

Why was the relinquishing of suffering so difficult?

'Can you appreciate yourself with more maturity?' he went on. 'Junk the weak victim part. Stop prophetically expecting the black hole. You expect yourself to be boxed in and then, sometimes, you are. Move beyond a child's-eye view, beyond the black and white, the sectarian. Integrate the polarities. *Know* that this is a spiritual world. You don't have to do anything. You're appreciated and loved *just for being you.* You have this ability to hear criticism and hostility without also hearing the respect and compassion on offer. Think of the number of people in the group who worry about you. Like me, the group gets frustrated. They recognise how much you suffer and how needlessly self-indulgent that is. Be humble. Be fair to others. Take responsibility. A death is required. Give up suffering.'

After nearly a year of reflecting on forgiveness and self-forgiveness at Eckhart House, in May 1994 I decided to write to Peter, to say what I needed to say and to wish him well. All I asked was that Peter would confirm that he had read my letter.

On Monday I told J what I had done. The couch session was pervaded with his usual concentration. It was only at the end that he sighed, as if murmuring a private thought, not intended for my hearing. 'I *do* hope he writes back.'

I was more moved by the humanity of those simple words than by his intellectually inspired interpretations over the previous year. J was no longer philosophising from a temple top about the psycho-spiritual meaning of love and loss. He was willing to come alongside me on this lonely earth. Maybe there would be no response. We were united in waiting and hoping for forgiveness.

A fortnight later, the three of us – J, the couch and me – met in our private dell, where I read out Peter's reply. And, finally, I chose to draw a line and to let go.

The foundation course in psychosynthesis was culminating in a week's summer school. Miceál, the Director of Eckhart House, had introduced the different methods of understanding the mystery of a human story through chronological events (*chronos*) or defining moments of change (*kairos*).

He invited each of us to close our eyes and to go inside, to imagine an ocean and to seek out the one wave that represented the individual life story that wanted to express itself through the opening line, 'Once upon a time ...'

Afterwards, I sat in the garden and wrote.

When we gathered again, Miceál encouraged us to share our stories aloud. His accompanying words were wise: rather than become entangled in comparison, we could see our contributions as part of one big weft, where every element helped to form the whole. So one voice after another began: 'Once upon a time ...'

It was one of those epiphanies where the beauty of the world was clear. Each story was distinctive and individual yet together they interlocked to form a universal story that was both aesthetically pleasing and spiritually moving. It was like seeing the patterning of snowflakes where previously there had just been snow.

I chose to read out my own story. I read about a lost little waterfall who did not think herself beautiful, who hid against an isolated mountain, so elevated that no one ever visited. But one day a climber had come along and stopped to gaze at her. He had washed his hands in her waters – a shocking, touching experience – and promised that he would come back. The waterfall had been afraid to hope, afraid to be disappointed again, yet the climber had faithfully returned, week in, week out.

Some days he cleared the leaves that clogged her flow; other times he helped her seek out her source.

One day, he told her, 'I think you are beautiful.'

The waterfall started to look at herself differently, to value her own colours.

The rocks, which had been silent for years, were intrigued. They asked her, 'What is happening?' The waterfall told them of her loneliness and showed them her tears. As she did so, the quality of her water became purer. The feeling of abandonment, of being alone, was lifting.

Now the time was coming when the waterfall wanted to free the climber of his commitment to her. The climber had given the waterfall the gift of love, and the waterfall knew it. Love had changed the waterfall. The story ended with the soul of the waterfall running down to the sea.

The following Monday, I read my story aloud to J from the couch, hoping that he would also hear my appreciation of him and our work. How he worked with the story was the best of him, revealing his intuitive ability to connect with the original wounded child and to elicit rich levels of meaning. That evening, as encouraged by J, I read aloud my story again in the group. More responses were added.

Not long afterwards, before J's office was due to close for the summer, I had a brainwave. I would ask my artistic aunt to paint a waterfall as a gift for J. At the outset of the last couch session before the break, I gave him the painting.

J seemed pleased enough. Encouraged by how well things were going between us, I ventured, 'What do you think of my letter-writing?' I had never before had the courage to ask but had been heartened by the recent openness between us.

'Which aspect do you mean? Your letters are so …' J hesitated, and the word dropped like a stone, 'voluminous.'

A slide into the cruellest of dynamics was starting up. A cool, metallic distance was coming between us, after a time of great intimacy. I was losing my confidence.

'Just an overview,' I said.

J edged out guardedly, 'Sometimes I feel anxious when you're writing late at night. I wish you were sleeping.' Silence. His tone sounded irritated. 'I feel you want a literary criticism from me. What do you want me to say?'

He was reverting to the tower of his withholding self, depriving me of a personal response because he relished having the power to withhold it.

Closeness was draining out the door.

He issued an academic summation. 'You write to convey feelings.'

The words dangled. He was determined to add nothing else. Bleak despair rose within me. I had been writing to him for six years; not one single word had affected him as a human being. A wracked sense of my own inadequacy and meaninglessness entered. The painting lay ruined.

'You are doing this to yourself again, hurting yourself.'

He was misinterpreting my most sensitive material, in order to avoid responsibility for what was happening in the room.

'Are we going to end like this?' J asked.

We did.

That night I was so upset, I could not sleep. The only thing I could think of was to get up early and wait outside his office on the chance that I might catch him before his first appointment. After an hour's wait, he came along. We stood in the morning street, and I told him how I felt. He listened, his sorrowful face showing that he took in my words.

'I'm sorry I hurt you,' J said. 'I'll have to think about what you've said, consider a more authentic reaction.'

There was nothing more we could do. He had his work to go to, as did I. He held out his hand for a handshake.

'Will we leave as friends?' he asked.

It was a striking phrase to use when he was usually keen to reinforce that he was *not* my friend, *not* my lover, he was my *therapist*. I felt his goodwill and extended my hand too.

That summer was long.

8

Lightness

i thank You God for most this amazing
day: for the leaping greenly spirits of trees
and a blue true dream of sky;and for everything
which is natural which is infinite which is yes

(i who have died am alive again today,
and this is the sun's birthday;this is the birth
day of life and of love and wings:and of the gay
great happening illimitably earth)

e.e. cummings

IF WE had met anywhere else, Damien and I would have relegated each other to the can't-stand-you category of people. But, in the group, we had to grapple beyond superficial judgements and destructive projections. I never managed to redeem my relationship with Tom;

with Damien I did. For his leave-taking, I bought him a ceramic oil-burner, hoping that when he was enveloped in scent, he would remember he was held by the loving feminine.

However, on Damien's last evening, I could not remember that for myself, murmuring dejectedly that I loved all wrong. Carol asked, 'There can be an immature, demanding love, but how can you love wrong?'

'When it's not reciprocated.'

She leaned forward, as if she understood. 'It's OK to have fantasies.'

Vera thought that the long-standing group members knew how to love, to show love.

Mark said to me, 'You've always been in relationship with the men here. You respond every time with courage.' My heart was soothed. He went on, 'Couldn't you bring down your defences, let someone in?'

Jeff agreed. 'You can have your intense connection with J and love other people as well. But it means you've got to go out and make an effort.'

Eva and I both had parting gifts for Damien. When mine was unwrapped, the burner was revealed – broken in smithereens.

I began to cry: 'It's a symbol of my love.'

Eva responded. 'You're doing it again, inflicting things on yourself, hearing and misinterpreting things against yourself. You're the only one telling yourself this. No one else is.' She added, 'Don't you know how much the group cares for you? You inspire such loving feelings here. I worry about you. We're not getting to the root of the problem. We've got to get there soon.'

Damien chimed in, 'Maybe she needs to give therapy a miss for a while.'

'No.' Eva said. 'She can do it.'

After another distressing group, I convinced myself that I could spend the night in J's waiting room, my adult thinking self once more overwhelmed by a frantic-feeling child. An hour and a half must have passed before I heard lights being switched off next door, then footsteps fading, when, for some reason, they turned back. The waiting-room door opened.

'Goodness! Have you been here all this time in the dark? You must be cold.' J looked concerned and refused to leave unless I came with him. As we walked down the stairs, he said, 'I will go with you as far as I can, but there is a part of the way you must go alone.'

My heart sank – why had he promised he would never leave me? Yet I also recognised a truth in his words.

'Have you got a teddy at home?'

I shook my head.

'I'll bring you in one of mine then.'

The man relished terms such as 'dyad' and 'ouroboros', but he also made room for spontaneous loving gestures and teddy bears. He referred to a book he was reading that he thought might help me. Plato? Ovid? No. William Horwood's *Duncton Tales,* the adventures of a mole on a heroic pilgrimage.

Not long after, I brought in the Big Dream. It had been galvanised by the long, hard labour of depression, welling up from that ever-present life spring that wants to offer support, if invoked and allowed. The nightmare's malevolent presence pursued me on the couch: the murderous cat screeching, her claws digging into my neck, and me sick with terror, desperate to shake off the hateful beast, yet, the more I tried to run away, the more she gripped on for dear life.

'Are you willing to work with the dream?' J asks.

I have become increasingly conscious of J's emphasis on will and choice, his encouragement to not be buffeted about by compelling unconscious drives. I can develop a stronger inner centre through the practice of meditation. I have also learnt that it is possible to sculpt a dream like clay and release inner wisdom. I tell J that I am willing.

'Close your eyes. Become aware of your breathing. Now I would invite you to step back into the dream.'

J feels like my protector, as well as soul guide, as we find ourselves back in my childhood bedroom opposite the police station, the one I keep revisiting in dreamland, as though wanting to show him something. J says that individual sessions often have the feeling quality of a girl crying alone in her bedroom.

J asks, 'Where is the cat?'

'Pacing by the window.'

'Where are you?'

'By my bed. I'm looking at her. She hates me. We hate each other.'

'Tell the cat you mean her no harm, that you only want to talk.'

I follow his advice.

J asks, 'What is happening?'

I hesitate. 'The cat is ...' – the electrifying truth of how it is – '... petrified.'

'Can the cat speak?'

'No. She's too frightened.'

In the cat's pupils, I see my own reflected. I understand her message. 'I mustn't touch her.'

The cat is shivering, seems sick.

'Could you get her some milk?'

The cat cautiously laps the bowl I place in front of her.

'Can you ask her why she's frightened?'

'No. That's too intrusive.'

The cat washes her paws, then looks up at me sadly. She mouths 'You know who I am,' and, in the transcendent purity of the dream-space, I do. There comes an hour when there is nowhere else to run, when you have to face yourself.

The attacking part of me has crept into J's room when the timing was right and she was able.

J asks gently, 'Could you ask the cat what she needs?'

The cat's innocent face considers my question.

'She says ...' – it is hard to get her words out – '... could I please stop attacking her.'

'Poor little cat. All this time she has been frightened when what she really wanted was to be in relationship with you.'

I am crying.

'What do you need?'

'Stroke my hair.'

'Ask the cat for help. See can you get what you need.'

I am so ashamed and so afraid of the attacking bit of me. The cat places one paw on my lap. I feel moved, knowing how brave this is, when the scarred animal finds it hard to touch or be touched.

J suggests, 'Would the cat like a stroke now?'

Her eyes convey: 'A tiny bit.'

I want to instil as much compassion as is possible into my hand, as though this is the most important caress there has ever been. I stroke the cat's trembling head and tense body.

The cat purrs.

For a long time, J and I rested in the aftermath of the beautiful dream work, like watching ripples together on a shore at dusk.

In the following couch session, I placed a lifelike object at the foot of J's armchair. The toy cat had marmalade fur, a red ribbon, white paws and a pink felt nose. J's face immediately lit up with a smile. He stretched down and lifted the cat into the air, as if it was a newborn baby to be cooed over. He scrutinised her features, gave her a long affectionate stroke and placed her back on the floor.

'Isn't she gorgeous?' he said.

I cuddled the cat in my arms, pleased at his response.

'I thought it best to get something for myself.'

'I thought the same afterwards.'

We were settling down companionably, going to work together with the cat for many months. J and I had forged a therapy that was sturdy enough to include many types of creative exploration, a fabulous freedom. And I had heard the dream's call to healing, had experienced an invaluable ally – if only I could befriend this wounded part of myself.

I have received an exceptional professional invitation to attend a world summit on children's television in Australia.

I cannot go. I have therapy three times a week. It is then that I see the rigidity J has been pointing out for years: how I lock onto agreements as overcompensation for an earlier, ever-shifting world.

'Talk to the group,' J suggests.

The group is unanimous: they are proud of me.

J is willing to offer my session times to other people meaning I will not have to pay, meaning he really does want me to have pleasure. After over six years of practically never missing a session, I am being released for three whole weeks, being let go lovingly – how important – and it is at my instigation, not J's. There is excitement inside, as if I am heading off to the Gaeltacht again, with hope in my heart that this time I will manage the transition to womanhood.

The summit is fantastic, and afterwards I travel on to Port Douglas on the Great Barrier Reef. For miles there is burning sun, azure sky and glistening water. Snorkelling is another sensual delight that my mind insists will not come naturally to me.

'The unknown is simply the unknown. You don't have to make it frightening.' (J and I have imaginary conversations even when he is not there.)

'If you get into trouble,' offers the tour leader. 'I'll swim out to help.'

That is all I need: the mothering figure watching over me. When I submerge my head, I blink at the vividness of the Reef, the shock that there is indeed another world beneath the surface. A disco queen of a fish shimmies up, her hue the essence of yellow, darting into the pink and purple coral sculptures. Everywhere is exhilarating vitality. This is like the surreal unconscious, teeming with energy.

The coral fans out into clumps, the sea floor shelving into blackness. J had warned us on that first psychosynthesis weekend, 'Choose your guide to the underworld carefully.' I had experienced for myself the dark energies in the unconscious, had drifted perilously close to eddying pockets that might have sucked me in. J had done his best to steer me from danger: 'Don't look down at yourself. Look up. Look out. Connect to others.'

Back on the boat, I get a fit of the giggles. The tour guide says, 'Some people have a nervous reaction after snorkelling.' I want to exult, 'Don't you understand? I'm alive! Life can be good! Life's to be enjoyed!'

When I was little, I gave the special feeling of happiness a name. I would be practising Irish dancing or thinking of something happy when my mother would ask, 'What are you doing?' I would be standing still, stretching out both arms and scrunching every muscle to let the excitement pass through. For a few seconds I would shake uncontrollably. 'It's the Grange Park feeling.'

My friends lived on a modest estate called Grange Park. They didn't have a separate bedroom or a garden or anything. Sometimes I would stay over. We would play in a sandpit, have chips for tea and exchange silliness until we fell asleep. It was the happiest place in the world. Over the years, the special feeling had disappeared into a hole. But that day, celebrating on the boat, I felt a thrilling reconnection with the sheer Grange Park-ness of Life.

Carol was absent the evening I returned to the group, but the others coaxed 'Go on, tell us,' as if I was the official adventurer for them all. So I did, but I could not convey the inner freedom that I had experienced. I had been alone, yet not lonely, had adored the space to travel and reflect in the luminous light of Australia.

A waterfall tour near Cape Tribulation had been a highlight of the trip. That night, we strangers had had to link hands to guide each other back to camp. I had found myself thinking of the group, and I realised that I was thinking of them with love.

What had changed? It was so subtle that it was hard to distinguish the contributing elements.

A recent interaction had certainly been important. Noel, fed up, had put it to me straight: 'It's impossible to say anything to you because everyone's afraid you'll run away. You're always walking out.' In his voice I could hear the honest exasperation of care, combined with the unflinching delivery of a hugely unpalatable truth.

Some comments hit because they come at an hour of readiness. Noel had said his piece after I had decided not to go further with the course at Eckhart House. A tutor there had commented to me, 'I'm struck at the violence with which you treat yourself.' I knew then that the right action was to come home to Belfast to resolve my problems.

I told Noel, 'I'm sorry. I promise I won't leave again.'

I was as good as my word.

Mostly, I thought the change was due to the work that J and I had been painstakingly crafting with the cat on the couch. The more I talked about the attacking part of me – inspired by J's compassion towards the poorly cat – the stronger I felt inside. The group was going better. I was being more open, realising that the attack I dreaded would be generated from inside of me.

I had sent the group a postcard from Australia, and now I gave each member a small, framed Aborigine draw- ing. The moment would have passed over quickly, except J astutely invited: 'Perhaps each gift has a meaning for you.' It became a great opportunity to express why I had chosen the turtle for Vera, the red snapper for Mark and so on. It opened up a new conversation about how we felt for each other.

Finally, when we were on our own, J also received his individual present. Having dithered about buying him a boomerang – he did love his theory about 'that which is repressed seeking to return like a boomerang' – I had settled on the quirkier gift of two Aborigine percussion sticks. I liked to think of him humming and tapping a good-hearted tune as he waited for his next patient to arrive.

Letter extract, 24 April 1995
Our journey has moved me, J. You have touched my soul. I want to know more about the nature of suffering and joy, spirit and soul, the journey of healing. If I must change, so must you, your perception of me as dark, complex, intense. Is that the cement between us? Does joy mean I must leave your space? Maybe I wanted to show you my courage by my capacity to suffer.

I want you to know and like a joyful me before I leave. Train me in a joy that will not deny suffering. Teach me about love that will not deny darkness. Nurture a lightness that will bring out the best in both you and me.

One day, after working together for a very long time, I came to know that the Master was a wounded warrior, that all of us are wounded.

I was vaguely aware of a strange idea rising in my head, the thought that if only one of us could be well, I wanted it to be J. Then, one day, when J was talking, an insight flashed across my couch mind. I realised – how could I not have seen this before? – that we were both wounded in exactly the same way; that, underneath the seeming disparities, we were uncannily alike at the roots. I saw the shape of his wounds. I saw how I mirrored his inner wounding back to him.

So I told him.

In our next session, he said, 'You stopped me in my tracks with your comment.'

It was one of those privileged moments of therapist–patient privacy, when our basic fault lines were revealed to each other in reciprocal confidence. After that, I think, the connection between us changed, deepened.

Talking about the feeling of eternal homelessness was like talking about brushing my teeth: it was a banal given. Other people had a right to security, not me. I had been trying to buy a flat and would return from viewing properties feeling down. I worried about the money, particularly since the fees for therapy were now equivalent to a small mortgage.

I decided to ask my father for the loan of a deposit on an apartment. My father quizzed me as to what I did with my own money and looked crestfallen when I proffered a non-committal reply. I had evidently failed him in his life-long teaching of discipline and determination. I wanted to let him get to know the real me. Maybe I, too, could know my parents as real people, people who made the best decisions they could, in demanding circumstances, and with their own wounding. I could tell my father that I *did* use everything he had taught me in order to pay my own way in therapy, to never give up. But I imagined he would be distressed, so I said nothing.

A few months later, I was at my parents' house again – I saw them more often now – when they came into the sitting room.

'We helped your sister, and we'll help you.' They wanted to communicate a message: we love you equally. 'Our one condition is it's to be used towards buying a flat.'

'OK.'

'And it's a gift, not a loan.'

And when I saw the cheque, I realised that, consciously or unconsciously, my parents did know about therapy. The figure was equal to six years' fees with J.

I talked to J about the inner part of myself I called the 'shattered self'. One day J suggested that we could tape a psychosynthesis meditation in an individual session, which I could then replay when alone.

'Focus on your breathing: not altering it, simply observing the breath. Let the breath take you inside to a quiet centre within. Breathing out, say to yourself: let go.'

J's voice on the recording sets a meditative rhythm.

'Remembering that in imagination all things are possible, you find yourself standing in a meadow. Hear the birds singing. Smell the scent of the grass.'

I have not thought of the daisy field beside my primary school for years.

'Imagine' – the voice sounds supportive – 'that you have the pieces of your shattered self with you.'

The shattered self takes the form of shredded tissues, mixed up with tears, broken glass and menstrual blood.

'Be aware of how you're feeling, what it's like to have a shattered self.'

It is awful.

'We are going to make a trip up the mountain to where the Wise Person is reputed to live. Find a way to bring your shattered self with you.'

There is a waxy plant whose leaves will make a knapsack. I place the mess in its centre.

'Be aware of how easy or difficult it is to manage this journey.'

It is very, very difficult.

'Climb the mountain, going higher, as the air becomes purer.'

J knows how to pace the meditation. The weight of the world is on my shoulders, so my ascent is slow. Curious how heavy these tissues are.

'Gradually the summit comes into view. Rest for a moment.'

I am grateful to leave my shattered self down.

'You notice a building and recall that this is the Temple of Silence. You determine to enter it to speak with the Wise Person. Pick up your burden. From high in the ceiling falls a shaft of sunlight. Where the light touches the ground, you notice a vessel. Resolve to place the shattered pieces into the container, to be worked upon by the golden light. As you do so, be alert. Wait. Watch for another image to emerge.'

This is where my despair starts. What if I am left alone, with no help on hand? There is the memory of J's steadying counsel: 'Be patient. Be open. Be receptive.'

The bloodied mass is transforming into a red poppy.

'Let the image develop until you see it clearly. Observe it closely.'

The flower is perfect.

'Be aware of how you feel about this image.'

I have a sense of awe.

'Be aware of being watched by the Wise Person. Don't be afraid. Feel yourself immersed in waves of love and understanding. The Wise Person may take the form of a man, woman, child, animal or object whom you may or may not see. Trust that the Wise Person is there and will communicate with you, if not now, perhaps in a dream, or in an unguarded thought. Take a moment to tell the Wise Person how things have been for you.'

Perhaps a well-intentioned gesture is going awry because the Wise Person is starting to look remarkably like J – the two are merging as I listen to the meditation repeatedly – and the erroneous sense is gathering in my psyche that the Wise Person is sited in J, not within me.

I tell the Wise Person that outside are the smashed-up 'Troubles', and inside I am heartbroken, struggling with the coming of womanhood. The Wise Person advises,

'Touch the poppy.' I delicately cup the flower in my hands and trace each petal. Up close I see the poppy's majestic features. She grows from a shattered mess of menstrual blood, and tears, and broken glass, but she blooms strong, and unafraid, and beautiful.

'In a moment we are going to leave. Ask the Wise Person for any advice.'

No. I have enough.

'Thank the Wise Person, knowing you can go back at any time. Then start your return, taking your new image with you. Be aware of how you feel.'

More hopeful.

'When you are ready, come back into the room.'

'There's still that pain-in-the-neck, self-absorbed, unre- sponsive bit of you.'

Yup, there he goes again in a couch session.

'The tragedy queen, living out of the hurly-burly of life. Yes, there has been real tragedy, a grievous harming, but you're not as intense as you were. You've learnt to analyse better, are framing things differently. Can you take on the philosophical plane, the spiritual dimension, move from the sombre quality of darkness to the essence? The group was asking you to bring in your colour, your light- ness and humour. They wanted to play with you. Can you honour them by hearing what they were saying, by not taking in the words as negative feedback, which links back to the internal attacking part? Can you give up the grief, relinquish these cycles of defeat and despair and allow the healing to come? Because, you know, there's a precious quality to you.'

Precious? What the hell does he mean? Is it another self-indulgent failing to be worked on?

'No, precious as in rare.'

As I walk through the fields, I think of those explorers who undertake death-defying expeditions. This is my Everest, but it is relatively ordinary. I have not mentioned my plan to anyone, in case my courage evaporates. I have to act first, and then know.

To an outsider, I can see that this location is impressive. That is why my father loved it: the uninterrupted landscape, the nearby lake and fairy fort. I look up and glimpse the rear of our old home. A chilling thought instantly surges in: 'That house is evil.'

I follow the track into the main street of the town. There it is, the grey-walled survivor, the inviolate police station. I turn around. Home. In the late sixties it was a state-of-the-art, split-level house. Now it looks sunken, having been rebuilt to accentuate drab functionality. A plump, moon-faced girl answers the door, like meeting myself from an earlier era.

'I know this'll sound odd. I used to live here and would like to say goodbye. Would you mind if I walked around the garden?'

'No problem. Do you want to come in as well?'

'No, thanks.'

I am choosing to go gently, to treat myself with kindness.

My father's garden, his pride and joy, is gone, as are the tennis court and the summerhouse. Once, every hour of available daylight, he used to be tending to ponds with lilies, designing flowerbeds with roses of every colour, making patios out of imported hexagonal slabs that arrived in a lorry. Every plant was referred to by its proper Latin name. In the evenings he could be found mowing his immaculate lawn. There were flowers in that garden I am sure were to be found nowhere else in Ireland.

Presents were easy: a gardening book, or a plant, if you did not have enough pocket money. Life revolved around the garden and its associated rituals. We would sit at the dinner table listening to BBC Radio 4's *Gardeners' Question Time* as if it was Sunday mass. My father would give the correct answers, quick as a flash before those high-falutin' English panellists. My father loved that garden like a child, like a lover, like a god.

When the dream was destroyed, for a long while you could not mention anything to do with gardening. Daddy seemed to slip away into depression.

I start my pilgrim's trail around the grounds of the house – remembering, grieving and mourning. The rose beds are covered in concrete. There is no pool, no vibrant orange fish. Only one tree has escaped the urban lava flow. God bless trees; they keep on going. At the foot of the remaining tree I bury the handful of torn black art paper I had put into my pocket, my symbol of the suffering from the past. I am leaving it all behind.

There is a second part to my soul-making ritual, for this is what I am doing. I want to visit the nearby ancient burial cairn that has repeatedly surfaced in psychosynthesis meditations. I drive through country roads I have not seen for years, stop the car near a decrepit moss-covered sign and start climbing up into the forest. There is no sound here other than the forlorn drizzle of rain trickling over leaves and the rustle of creatures burrowing. After I have walked for an hour, a clearing in the woods reveals a blue-purple blanket of wild bluebells. I stop to breathe in its beauty and then continue on. Finally the cairn appears, with its imposing presence that had impressed me as a child.

I have brought more art paper with me. At the burial chamber I make tiny envelopes, fill them with coloured shapes, each one symbolising a person from the group, both past and current. Into each envelope I scatter rose petals mixed with black paper, symbol of our shared hope and heartache. I deliver the envelopes to the cairn and say a prayer for our well-being.

Then I begin my descent. I am a gardener's daughter and know that to collect wild flowers is wrong, but this is an exceptional day, and the woodland gods approve of their purpose. I pick sheaves of glorious bluebells. When I return to Belfast, I drive to an unfamiliar address and open a new door.

This was the motivation for my cleansing ritual. I have bought a flat!

The past is the past. I am committing to something good and happy for me, trusting that the world can be re-imagined. I have devoted myself to creating a safe inner sanctuary – the task of Sisyphus – and a home has also materialised in the external world. I unpack the chimes I bought a year ago – my symbol of lightness when lightness seemed impossible – and hang them in my sweet garden. With champagne, I christen my flat 'Aerach' – Irish for 'Lightness'. I think to myself, *May I not die tonight, so that he may know the joy of our work.*

The next morning, the bluebells looked wiltingly ordinary. On the couch I gave an account of my ritual and then unexpectedly swivelled around with the flowers.

'You see, these are for you. They are a thank-you present, from one sacred place to another.'

But I had surprised J with my sudden move, because I saw – and maybe I got this wrong – that J was crying.

It was precisely seven hours later that J felt prompted to comment in the group about my inability to play, my intensity, my seriousness. That was all he said about me.

I felt searingly hurt: the pain, the pain of intimacy pushed away (again), the price for coming too near; the split between individual sessions (hidden, private, loving) and the group (confrontational, unyielding, berating); his toughness on me, pushing me towards an exacting stand-ard no one else seemed obliged to reach; and the sorrow that he could never see me in any other way.

In 1995, approaching my seventh summer in therapy, J confides that he is like me: he finds it hard to love. I feel moved that he too knows the longing to love, yet the ter-ror of love.

Then he says, 'I love you.'

My agitated response takes me aback. 'No. You mustn't talk about love. I'm no good at love. My love is meaningless. It has no power.'

Now it is the first day after the summer break, and the familiar ecology of J's consulting room is disturbed by two additions. The first, a framed award, beams out professional pride: *honorary*, *diploma*, *services*. The second, a large photographic portrait of a beautiful woman, dominates the far wall. She seems to have been placed strategically so that whenever J opens his eyes from analytic reveries he will see her. I study her features.

'Who is she?'

A moment's hesitation, then he utters what I already intuitively know. 'She is my wife.'

The rest of the session crumbles away. There have been problems at work. I want sympathetic stroking; J embarks on a moralising trail about acting from a place of ego. So he can enjoy a prestigious career, while the rest of us mere mortals are to be castigated.

The group is another god-awful evening. I am complaining about the earlier individual session. J is riled, sensing that I am out to undermine him. He believed that he was being supportive earlier and seemingly invites the others to speak up about their difficulties with me. I am furious, hearing him using his therapist's power to manipulate the others into articulating his resentment of me. He has won. He always has to be the perfect therapist whom no one can criticise.

Rage floods the next couch session.

'Did you pity me? Is that why you said you loved me?'

And now I remembered having once read that the Persians have eighty words for love and realised that, before the summer, J had used Persian word No. 67 and that I had heard Persian word No. 3.

'This was the one space that was for me. But you don't want to look at me, do you? You want to look at *her*.'

'Aren't you always asking me for more of the feminine in here?'

So his wife represents the archetypal feminine to which I am to aspire, and I am to bring in my useless attempts at love – the agony of which he will never know – and lay them out before the adoring couple. I could kill him. J concedes that he did not reflect too much on the potential impact of his actions. This is from the King of Interpretations, who mines every wayward sigh for meaning.

Well, it's done now.

The following Monday morning, I saw what had happened, so why did I feign blindness and keep on going with my couch tirade? At the end, J sounded cutting. 'If you took the time to look, you would see that the portrait is gone.'

That evening, group members wondered why the two room additions had disappeared. Eventually I confessed, it was me. I was the mean, jealous one. I was the one who got exposed in my ridiculous yearning and had loved all wrong again. That night I left several distraught messages on J's answering machine. 'I want you to put the portrait back.' Early the next morning I slipped a note under his door: 'I don't have the courage for therapy any more. You would be better off with someone who understands the complexity of the human heart, who doesn't make the stupid mistakes I do.'

J made a rare gesture. He left a friendly message on my answering machine. 'I don't blame you. Not at all. You've had great bravery to speak up. Come along and we can talk about it.'

It was just another day – another day when I was intent on provoking J out of his basket, like a daring mouse teasing a cat, so that his every nerve would quiver and we would spin our well-worn game of intimate friction. The pattern was swelling into its usual crescendo, me in a scathing rant, when he pronounced my name in a tone that was almost kind.

'You don't have to do this. This aggression is unauthentic. It is not the anger between adults. It is a misrepresentation, a way of setting me up and treating me like an object.' He sounds firm but not cross, as if he is rejecting the anger but not me. As if he is on to me. 'This has to stop.'

And just like that – wallop! – in sweeps the twisting, sick feeling. With a shock I realise that the symptom that catapulted me into therapy has never once been between us as a lived experience; it has only ever been reported. J seems suddenly intensely physically close. I feel faint. J says quietly, 'I don't want to shame you.'

The shame of being so frightened, of being stripped bare in fear. J sees me as I am. He is not going to leave me.

Silence. Silence. Silence.

At last I find my voice: 'I'm terrified of love.'

What a quixotic thing to say, yet I feel alive to myself in saying it, as if I am making meaning for me, for the two of us, in this moment.

'I can understand that.'

J is not judging me. I feel little and lost. Another realisation rolls in: that, unconsciously, I have done everything to keep this terror out of therapy. Nothing can survive this scythe of a feeling. Anger has been my strategy for managing the unbearable intimacy of the therapeutic situation.

'I'm terrified of being real.' It is another bizarre statement, but, again, I feel real to myself in saying it.

'I am feeling for you. Can you feel my heart open to you?'

I know I could wreck this moment, crank up another row, but – and this is hard – I do not want to do it.

J says, 'I love you for who you are. Be real for who you are.'

Inside I think, *Have I never been real before now?*

J encourages, 'Talk about your unrequited love for me.'

I stumbled as the session ended, so I sat in the waiting room with my head between my knees, until the faintness passed. It took a while before the out-of-date Miró calendar came into focus and the faded piles of *Newsweek*s and *London Review of Books*. Then I did what I always did to contain feelings: I wrote.

That evening, J and I shared with the group what had been happening. I heard him saying – he sounded loving – that I could not meet him in the way we both wanted, out of terror, but that my terror had a meaning.

I felt fantastic inner hope. I was thinking, *I'm not going to go on hiding my terror and my love. I want to be visible.*

However, forty minutes later, J turned and pronounced to me in front of everyone, 'I am bored with your repetitious story.'

And the crushing cycle started all over again.

Letter extract, 8 January 1996
Was I ever real? Did I dream that attempt by both of us to be real to each other in a loving-frightening way? I could cope with your anger

and rejection if it wasn't always preceded by an encouragement to love. If we could agree a consistent line, then presumably neither of us would get hurt. I can only speak for myself. I hurt deeply about it all. It feels like a physical pain, an ache in my heart. It is so cruel.

Are you afraid that I would love you? I was willing to move away from anger, to be terrifyingly real. Somehow, I experienced that you preferred things the way they were. Over and over we repeat something very wounded, wounding and painful. I am conscious that we will soon begin our eighth year of working together. You often speak of redeeming what happens in the relationship between us. How is that possible unless we share an understanding of the meaning of what it is to be redeemed? For me this sequence is the hardest and most meaningful. I would like to understand the meaning of what happens between us.

9

The sun going down

Essentially, we might say, the cure is effected by love.

Sigmund Freud in a letter to Carl Jung, 1906

ISRAEL'S PRIME minister, Yitzhak Rabin, has been murdered. Shimon Peres is on the radio, his voice shaking with emotion, talking about how the road to peace is littered with setbacks and acts of terrorism. I am remembering group conversations about how hard it is to change, to make peace with oneself and with the world.

The unimaginable has happened in Northern Ireland: the IRA and the Combined Loyalist Military Command have announced ceasefires. Newspapers report the decommissioning of arms, the symbolic act of surrender in a land where symbols have assumed inordinate power because they have usurped the role of talking. Acres of print are given over to the story: is it possible that the arms will be rendered permanently unusable or are we going to be sold out again? International nominees are being driven to isolated farmhouses, where men in balaclavas display ingenious bomb-making material, constructed from the components of the domestic world.

Into J's room I brought a biscuit box, sealed tight with a lid. I had worked on my box all night long, filling it with objects, both real and symbolic, that I associated with the attacking part of me. I had to do my bit. I told J, 'These are my arms for decommissioning. I'm handing them over to you.'

At the end of the session, J sounded awestruck. 'Are you sure you want to leave your box with me?' It was as if he was saying, how could you possibly entrust me with this sacred casket? His words were not trained, or learned, or borrowed from a book. He was speaking from his heart, believing in the value of our work, honouring me with that mighty quartet: faith, love, respect and dignity. He trusted me. He trusted me completely. In that moment, I loved him, and trusted him completely too.

For months we worked with the box. Each session I would take out one object: for example, a pristine white sanitary towel. I would tell J what had happened in the Gaeltacht, how my period had unexpectedly arrived and I had got into a total teenage panic because the sanitary towel would not flush away. I could not talk to anyone about it, because talking about periods was anguish for me. The solution was to sacrifice the hope of a first kiss and to return to the unsettled home where I could just about manage.

Each time, my heart was moved at J's refusal to brutalise the box's contents, his constant care. Then I realised, with sadness, that he was being to my box and to me how I could never be. I remembered themes from the group: how you can resist loving, reject whatever comfort is on offer, spoil the good and turn it into bad. I listened to J's words, 'Be loving to yourself. Be loving to the beast.'

I told the group about the self-hurting rituals during my late childhood and teenage years.

Eva responded, 'The penny's dropped.'

Mark nodded, 'I see something clearly now.'

Vera added, 'I could feel you shaking as you were speaking. I wanted to put out my hand to you.'

Jeff asked, 'How did you expect the group to react?'

I said that I was afraid that they would be shocked or horrified and would reject me.

Jeff continued in that rooted style of his. 'It's like a ritual for rehearsing a possible pain, isn't it? Like not allowing in criticism for fear of what is coming, so you get in first with self-criticism, get in with physical pain before emotional pain.' He felt like the spokesperson for the loving group I could at last let in.

'Do you know where your ideas about sex and pain came from?' Jeff asked, seeming energised. 'Could your father have unconsciously wanted to keep you to himself, in how he told you about sex?'

'No,' I replied, but it was liberating to allow in the possibility that people could unconsciously act in ways that their conscious mind might disavow.

The group zigzagged on, with talk of the victim and the torturer, the bully within, and – was it J who raised it? – the terror of another.

Eva said to me, 'There are so many different sides to you. You've got this vitality and persuasiveness.' (J has an infinitely less flattering term for it: 'drama queen'.) Hers was the last challenge to the others: 'The group can't leave the work to her any more. We've got to change.'

For the first few moments after entering J's room, I was disorientated. After years of obedience, the couch had made a mad dash for freedom. Its position had been changed. Now it was located at a slight diagonal to J's armchair, creating the option to either include J in your gaze (and vice versa) or to continue in the classical analytic way.

I immediately assumed that J was responding to the quantum leap I had made. I sat facing him, my feet tucked under my legs, delighted that he was open to this new phase of relating. It would be a lot of trouble for him moving the couch each time for the others, but that could not be helped.

That evening, when I sailed into the group, one voice after another spoke about the significance of the changed couch. I did not say a word. The pain, the pain of being stupid. The fury that J had not made the situation clear earlier, had not stopped me from going on happily. And, underneath, the yearning (again, again, again) that he would do something just for me.

I was once more on the verge of giving up, telling myself, *Sure, we go nowhere in the group, trudging around the same old problems.* But I did not. I had come to understand that the group was a powerful field of energy, affected by every person in it. The experience had also taught me that I could never know when some small shift might happen and the smallness might be enough to make a difference. So I had to hang on in there, keep faith, even when there seemed to be no reason for faith.

The group had been evolving, J growing as a more experienced therapist. He still strapped himself to the mast of his training, but he participated in a less formatted, predictable way. He was like a fish coming to know that he *was* a fish and could trust the natural current of the water. There was no longer that slightly artificial labouring over the mechanics of interventions.

The group, too, was changing. Carol had left. I missed her, but the group itself felt solid. Trust and depth were entering. The same configuration of people had been working together for two years; four of us had been alongside each other for four years. I was the most senior member, having participated for over six years. Somehow, this particular combination worked well, meaning that there was enough ballast, strength and capacity among us to engage with the analytic task.

Never had our maturity been more visible than when J had informed us that he could not attend one Monday. After much conversation, we had decided to meet anyway in J's office, by arrangement. We were so good that evening; we were shining.

Now, several weeks later, Noel is opening up the circle, having been overseas for the past fortnight, visiting his family. He says he appreciates that his relatives have done their best for him and mentions his favourite film, *Il Postino*, referring to it as a metaphor for love. There, like a boat floated out on a lake, is the evening's theme.

The others are bantering when Noel comments, 'Something seems to have happened in my absence.' Jeff turns to me, 'You've been silent this last while.' I stare at the carpet, like a prisoner on trial.

Usually J likes to listen for the first half of the group, to let the conversation build. Tonight he is getting involved early, urging me to speak up, but I cannot, and he knows why.

In all my years, I have never before seen what happens next: J asks for my permission to talk about what has been happening in our individual sessions. I nod, steeling myself. I have no defence against his brilliant intellect. I am merely a patient (from *patior,* meaning to suffer the slings and arrows of a therapist).

The group becomes silent. What has been going on? The tentative nature of J's tone strikes first, as if he is finding this hard. 'I want to speak from my perspective, to set what has been happening in a context that is fair.'

This is not the scaffolding of a confident therapist persona but a hesitant human being, attempting to be a therapist in new form.

'Eina has felt silenced by the intimacy between us. I am undertaking to break that. A few weeks ago, she spoke in the group about her sense of the relationship with me being like an affair.'

That evening I had summoned up the courage to speak publicly about my feelings of sexual yearning for J, to name the cavernous energy that did not belong in the external world but which, in the internal world, was intensely alive and consuming.

J goes on: 'At the end of the session, I said that if a relationship wasn't sexual, it wasn't an affair.'

You see, that same evening, another woman in the group had revealed that she *was* on the verge of a real-life affair, but, as yet, nothing explicitly sexual had happened. It was to her that J had addressed his remark. However, the entire group had risen up as one, challenging J to consider the implications of what he was saying for me. The group had grasped the power of my internal world. The person who did not understand was J.

'Afterwards, she had come along furious, feeling betrayed and denied.'

The cynic in me is bristling out of defensive fear; however, J seems unsure of himself. He is determined to go on. 'Initially my response had been to be angry. Then I thought, *Hang on, maybe she's got something here.* We were able to have a genuine meeting. We agreed we'd both speak to the group. The following Monday, other issues were directed towards me.'

I had silently waited and waited. He had not said a word. Then I knew J did not want to publicly state what he had been saying in individual sessions: that he loved me. But I could not tell the group this because it felt like a private confidence. I could not betray J.

'I began to think there was a truth in what she was saying,' J continued.

What is he doing? The others are listening intently.

'Earlier she told me that I would be triumphant.'

My comment in Monday's individual session had obviously hit home.

'I have no wish to triumph.' – *Pause.* – 'In the current climate there is a fear of abuse in the therapeutic context.' So that explains his anxiousness. 'We've worked together for a long time. We've gone through many things together. It's a very intimate relationship. I have feelings of tenderness for' – *Don't breathe.* – 'Eina. I've loving feelings for her. I care for her welfare. I love her.'

Have I heard right?

'I love her and I hate her.'

Always the way.

'I hate aspects of her. They drive me mad, make me irritable.' Another pause. 'But it's not a humanitarian love.'

Is he thinking of what I tossed at him in the earlier individual session? 'Why did you say you loved me when you knew how much that would mean to me? Why didn't you make it clear that you meant it like you love the whales? A sort of altruistic love. You didn't love *me*. Or was talking about love some clever technique you learnt on your training, only it didn't mean a thing?'

He speaks slowly. 'It is a love for *her*, a definite person. She has felt herself abandoned in life, betrayed and denied. She has suffered at the hands of others. It is important for her to feel loved, to know that she is loved, and for this to be spoken publicly. She needs to hear herself loved in the group. It is about seeing and being seen, being known as important. So, yes, here and now, I'm saying that I love her.'

I know the blast of near-death, yet this is the explosive shattering of life, of love. I feel stunned to my core. Members are commenting that what J had said, and how he has expressed himself, has been beautiful. J is surprised, adding that it was not like that as an experience for him. 'Maybe there is something powerful about speaking from within.'

Eva and Jeff are both asserting that they know the same love is on offer to them from J. It is through the security of their responses that I realise my own lack of confidence. I feel their love for J and me coming into the space in a new, more balanced way.

Eva turns to J. 'You know, J, I wish you'd only talked about the loving, given her some time just for loving, so she wouldn't have to cope with the hating as well.' It is Eva's comment that touches my heart – her understanding of my needs, her generosity of spirit.

Jeff says to J, 'You've modelled something important for me about therapeutic love.' He goes on to talk about his feelings towards his wife, how you can love someone and want to strangle them, how silence can be used as a weapon in a relationship. 'You seem more real, J,' he concludes.

Eva agrees. Then Jeff addresses a surprising comment to me. 'I've always felt the same about you as J has expressed. I've been attracted to you, but as you said yourself, your entire focus was directed towards J. There didn't seem any point in mentioning this before now. There didn't seem room for anyone else.'

I am taken aback. Must I release myself from this mesmeric trance, this electrifying binding in imagination to J? Are there men I have been oblivious to, good men I have been unavailable to, because, unconsciously, my heart and psyche are captured?

J turns to Mark: 'I wonder how you've heard what I said? How will you use the experience?' Mark replies with even-natured equilibrium. 'I'm impressed with you and with Eina – with her dignity.'

I feel as though my every last ounce has been engaged in a mud battle these past weeks, my hair flying in grizzled strands. There seemed little dignity about it, but is Mark pointing out aspects of me that I do not celebrate in myself?

Mark continues, 'Something has changed in you, J. There was something pivotal in you moving the couch. Tonight is evidence of that change.'

J reiterates that it had been important to speak about our relationship in the group, for it belongs to the whole group. The dynamic between him and me, Eva and Mark – which the two are discussing – are versions of the same thing. Where had the group Mother been in the midst of what had been happening between J and me? Why, time and again, J asked, had Mother not got involved? Father had been left to sort it out. Father had taken over. Why had the members let me continue to think of the relationship as an affair? Why was it only now that they were intervening out of love for the two of us?

Vera asks me, 'How do you feel about what J has said?'

If he stated that he loved me publicly, then the others would witness that I had the capacity to inspire love, that my love for a man, and his for me, would not be something shameful or fearful. I would have loved *properly* as a woman, because my unconscious anxiety is that it is *my fault* that I cannot feel the security of love back. I have gone to that inner terrain of shock where no words form. People might misunderstand my silence. I look across at J.

'Thank you. I think what you did was brave.'

Eva interjects, not prepared to let the opportunity go. 'It was *you* who was brave too.'

Members will tell you when you are being a brat. They will not collude with you 'doing a number', as J calls it. However, they can equally point out positive aspects that you need to take in for your own well-being. Sometimes it feels as if I have handed over my good qualities to J, so that I can see his but not my own.

There is more talk of what it is to be true and real, of people's experience of love. Eva says to J, 'You seem a bit irritated.' Instead of deflecting the question back for self-exploration, J replies, 'Actually, I feel passionate.' He refers to his daughters, how when they were young and he went away, he had to bring back each one a present. The theme is how can you show people that you love them equally yet differently.

J wants to check with me how had I heard his words about being loved and hated by him? I silently wonder: does referring to the hatred make the love safer or does including the hatred make the love more authentic? His hate has always been there; it is his love in action that has shocked me. I tell him that I can cope with both.

'What J has done is the ultimate confrontation, isn't it?' Eva comments. 'It means that from now on you'll have to take responsibility for yourself, stop going down those old paths.' Yes. I can choose to trust this experience of love or not. I can choose to let the love in.

Jeff muses, 'You often make me think of *The Antiques Roadshow*. It's as if you've been testing something to make sure it's authentic, but in doing so you've been destroying the picture.'

The group knows me well. The members seem freed by J's overt placing of trust in the group and are actively taking on collective responsibility for the analytic work. For J is reiterating: he and I do a lot of work for the group. Yes. I am a carrier, a catalyst. 'You impact,' J had once said to me individually. 'You're like me. People are not indifferent to you. That can sometimes be hard.'

Now J is sharing, 'It's difficult to say "I love you", isn't it? I know I find it difficult.' Then he turns to Eva. 'I love you.' He moves on to Mark. 'I love you.' And round the circle he goes, telling each person 'I love you.'

This is not an hour of evangelical schmaltz or whooping declaration. This is a breathtaking moment when J has broken away from the classical formality that makes him feel safe, in order to respond to a greater need. He has been afraid; he has done it anyway. Tonight he is being all of who he is, including his giftedness and woundedness.

He loves each of us.

And the group, indisputably, has a secure, loving place for me.

Three sets of heartbeats – Father, Mother and mine – pulse in harmony, an extraordinary beginning for life.

For years I have never really looked at J. What if he were to get knocked over when collecting his lunchtime sandwich? I imagine a crowd forming, me trundling along, policemen with notebooks, and someone from the hairdresser's pointing at me, 'Oh, *she'll* be able to identify him.' I imagine myself staring at the man's features and replying, 'Um, I'm sorry but ...'

In recent couch sessions I have found myself often thinking about blindness and Helen Keller. I have this desire to trace J's face with my fingers, to know him not as a phantom Father, Mother or Lover but as an embodied human self.

Now it is Thursday, and J and I are alone after Monday's stunning group.

There is a decisive moment of awakening in myths and fairytales when the heroine is released from a wicked spell by an act of love. J has put my needs before his own, has heard and responded to my soul's longing, has made me visible as one who is loved. Oh strange new world. No one is lost for ever.

He is taking me in, almost with curiosity. I am letting him do that. I can be seen. I am taking him in, this man who has astounded me. For I know him, not the minutiae that forms the substance of ordinary relationships but the osmotic knowing that flows between therapist and patient, meaning that in an identity parade of hearts, I could identify his anywhere. J too has a part that suffers, but he spoke up for me, for integrity. He could have used academic theory to protect himself from his own fears. No one would have been any the wiser, except me, and my reaction could have been explained away. J did not do it.

This is the beginning of the end of my secret imaginary affair with J, but the truth is it will take a long, long time to be over, such is its tenacious hold on my psyche. We are not lovers. We never have been; we never will be.

He has been my spirit lover, my darling beloved. Can't you see him? Isn't he precious? The man with whom I decided to practise loving, only loving proved bigger than me.

Paradoxically – yet there is no paradox – this is the closest moment there has ever been between us. What strikes me most is how I feel unafraid in my body. The sickness is gone. It is as if – absurd notion – J's public declaration of love was like a symbolic sexual union. I am ready. This intimacy is what my soul longs for, no matter what my mind tells me. After seven years of valiant work as therapist and patient, we are meeting as two ordinary people in an ordinary Belfast room, our truest selves. I see him. I *really* see him. And, in this moment, when I am called to let go, I feel a deep love for him *as J*, beyond what he has had to carry these long years. In return, I feel loved and seen by him.

He speaks first. 'I didn't want to triumph over you. Why would I? I didn't feel good about what had happened. I had to take a stand, put myself on the line for you. If I hadn't, I would have betrayed you. I couldn't do that to you. I had to do what others hadn't done in the past.'

All these years I had been seeking to salve a pain that was pressing on my heart. I had never understood what it meant; I had just kept on searching. Yet now I knew: I needed to experience myself being put first. As J studies me, an insight seems to click.

'You've always been a girl to me. I could never see you as a woman.'

I think of the new dresses I twirled before him, the haircuts I showed off, the yearning to be pretty, to be seen as a woman by him. He was oblivious to it all. I had never had that flirtatious relationship he sometimes enjoyed with other women in the group. He had never found me sexually attractive.

Even in this respect, something seems to be changing.

I do not understand what this means. All I know is that to be true to the love that is real, I must relinquish illusion. It is not fair on him, or me, any more. It is no longer – the words in my head are specific – *a moral act*.

This time, when we could share the best of ourselves, get to know each other, signals that the end of the therapy is nigh. I must begin to leave J at the point where love has been discovered. Eva is right. He cannot serve me any better. Responsibility for my life rests with me.

'The sun is going down,' J murmurs softly. 'Always the dawn and the dusk, something lost and gained. You must find your own man to love you in the way that you need. Discover for yourself the torment of love' – such a J thing to say. 'The therapy is ending.'

I know that this is true and cannot stop bittersweet tears from trickling down my face. J gently reassures me, knowing how terrified I get at even the concept of separation.

'We can take our time with this.'

An odd thought has entered my brain.

'I'll have to change my bank codes.'

A shocked look passes across J's face, but I do not want to hold anything back in what feels like our final hour. We can talk fully and share the secrets that have always been between us.

'You see, they're all linked to you. I knew I'd never forget them that way. You've been everything to me. You've been my life.'

It was before midnight when I committed to an act of will. 'Hello,' chirped the English banking voice. 'Can I take you through security? Can you give me the third letter from your password?'

The third letter of his first name.

'First letter?'

First letter of his name.

'Memorable address?'

His office address.

'Memorable date?'

The day I told J of Carmel's death.

It is too much to overturn a world of intense attachment. Tonight I am able to surrender only one code. I will give him back his name, the name I loved loving. The woman in the far-off call centre does not know the significance of my actions, but I do. 'Can you confirm your new password?'

First letter, A. *The dawn and the dusk.*

Second letter, L. *And everything entangled with spirit, with love and sorrow, death and resurrection, endings and beginnings.*

Third letter, I. *And it is all so exquisite, joyous, wonderful.*

Fourth letter, V. *And the sadness, the grieving, the loss.*

Fifth letter, E. *Yet the loving, the unbelievable loving.*

'Is your new password correct?'

The sun is going down.

'Yes, yes, that's it.'

10

Leave-taking

Ending is necessary if the analytic work is not to become a static alternative to a fully lived life.

Stephen Mitchell, *Hope and Dread in Psychoanalysis*
(1993)

'GOODNESS, WHATEVER has happened?'

J appears at his waiting-room door as I am hauling myself upright with a walking stick, my neck in a surgical collar, my leg swathed in bulky bandages.

'Jesus, that's some car crash you've been in,' the taxi driver had said when he had picked me up from the surgery earlier that morning.

'Complete bed rest' had been the medical instructions. However, I could not miss therapy, not after the two powerful sessions of the previous week. The only option had been to take a taxi straight to J's from the doctor's, to press the long-suffering solicitor's buzzer in order to gain access to the building and to lie flat on the waiting-room bench for nearly an hour.

A woman's voice had been faintly audible through the wall.

'You've an extraordinary life,' I had once told J. He had replied, 'Some people would find it boring.' Yet it is extraordinary to be party to so many confidences, to be the repository of whispered secrets and intimate tales of hurt, and somehow hold them all. How does he calmly say, 'It is time, but we can come back to this again,' when someone's innards are tumbling out and, five minutes later, be ready to attend to another person? What has he heard? Does he think about us patients outside his office hours?

I want someone loving to be by his side at night. I realise that I still want that more for him than for myself.

'Can I lean on you?'

When the arthritis had struck seven years ago, I did not have the confidence to ask for physical support. Now my hedgehog spikes have been mollified by hours of meticulous care. J stretches out a besuited arm, and I rest on him as we take restricted steps into his consulting room, linked arm in arm. It does not feel awkward. He feels old and reliable, but his steps are far too quick. I am the one who has to self-consciously laugh, 'Slow down.' No words will materialise on the couch to explain what has occurred. The thing is, I do not know.

Twenty-four hours after changing my bank password, I was on a bus, heading towards Seville for Easter with my cousin Anne. It was Good Friday.

She had asked, 'Well, any boyfriend?'

I had replied, 'No,' yet felt compelled to add, 'but I've had a profound experience of love.'

'Oh, that's grand then.'

As we travelled on, I was thinking about the wonder and the terror of ending therapy, the responsibility of loving myself, of being all that I could be. The sky was sinking into biblical gloom when, at precisely three o'clock, lightning ripped apart the plain. Then the rain descended, not just rain but a torrent of hailstones hammering the windows like a bereft lover, pleading for comfort.

He is gone.

The night streets of Seville swarmed with slit-eyed, hooded figures, assaulting the senses with death and resurrection tableaux: young men dragging crucifixes, marauders parading crowns of thorns and everywhere sickly incense. It was a relief to escape to Granada and the Alhambra, bathed in orange blossom. So this was what was possible in the name of love.

Forty-eight hours later I fell ill with a chronic arthritic attack and had to be flown home in a wheelchair.

Dr Hao is petite and elegant, with a welcoming smile. Her reception area has rows of what look like brandy-ball sweet jars, except that they are stuffed with seemingly pieces of bark. My GP has told me that I will have to be admitted to hospital if my condition does not improve. My friend Shirley, a shiatsu practitioner, has suggested Chinese medicine. That is how I come to be in this waiting room.

I feel nauseous as Dr Hao examines my swollen knee, turns my throbbing neck left and right. Then this woman, whom I have never met before, offers a striking assess-ment: 'Body has had a shock.'

My inner body leaps out in gratitude. She under-stands the shock I got when J overturned everything in the group.

'Body weak from shock.' Dr Hao is taking charge. 'No more work. No cook. Someone else cook. Must sleep. Drink herbs. Taste terrible. Good for body. Soon we try acupuncture.'

My mother drops everything to look after me with unstinting devotion. I need my mother. I want my mother – at last I can say it – and she is there for me. We are both older, edges sanded down, hearts and minds opened. Maybe we can get to know each other as friendly adults, negotiate a new way of being, for the past is the past and cannot be changed, but the relationship with the past, as I have discovered, can be transformed with inner work.

'This reminds me of when you were a baby. I'd sleep when you'd sleep,' she says, two beings bound up in inter-dependency.

Every morning my mother religiously follows Dr Hao's instructions. She boils the gnarled bark, lets the acrid smell billow over the kitchen and pours the vile drink into a glass, with honey on the side. At night she reads Isabel Allende's *Paula*, a book she has borrowed from me about a mother's love for her dying daughter. She sleeps on the sofa, calls in to me before switching off the light. She never complains. She says she loves this time to be close, even though she wants me to be well, says that this is one of the happiest times of her life. She enjoys getting to know my friends (and me), making tea, not being shut out. For years she has written me loving letters – sometimes two a week – always hoping that I would come back to her. Now I can stop punishing her, see her strengths and enjoy her company. Resting in bed, I can let a truth in: she loves me very much. And me her.

The last time I was ill, I would think resentfully, *The body has betrayed me.* This time, I am framing a new thought: *My body is helping me.* J had offered to take the ending of therapy off the agenda but, in my heart of hearts, I knew we could not. I kept limping along to sessions, but it was Dr Hao who dominated at this time. For I loved it when she inserted her tingling needles, turned the lights down low and sat by me, the sick child, like a Buddha Mother in a cave.

I have been confined to bed for nearly three months, yet all I feel is lucky. I am loved by J, and by the group, and by my mother. Sometimes my mother and I sit in my little walled garden, talking about her life and mine. When my mother returns home, she sends a letter confirming that our newfound relationship is a cherished gift.

As my health improves, I can acknowledge the work stress that contributed to the overall weakening of my health. I resign from the job I once adored. Every day I listen to one of four psychosynthesis meditations that J had recorded for me. This one ends, 'Take one small step.'

I remember meeting two broadcasters at the Australian summit and recall talk of a follow-up summit being planned for London. The same step keeps suggesting itself: write to them.

When I tell J in an individual session, he queries how realistic I am being about freelance work. His doubt connects me to the rational factors going against any such possibility: me being based in Belfast, the commuting costs, the competitive London market. So I do nothing. But the same thought persists. Finally, I decide I have nothing to lose. I have to follow my own intuition, no matter how unlikely it seems to anyone else, even my therapist.

Now, by July 1996, I have negotiated a six-month freelance consultancy, with the option to direct an exciting international children's television project and move to London in spring 1997.

I tell my friend Nuala that I may be leaving therapy soon and am touched by her reply: 'Maybe you're ready to love someone of your own.'

Only J is puzzled.

'Other patients end therapy without having to leave the country.'

But I know I have to make a major change in order not to turn back. My life in Belfast has been inextricably wrapped up with J and with therapy. A sacrificial price has to be paid.

Something is not right between J and me. I sense it. Have I fallen into that part of the labyrinth where the therapist is deliberately retracting his energy in order to prepare the patient for being alone? Or perhaps J enjoys the uncovering detective work and endings are a tedious bore. The shutters of his self feel boarded up for the winter. The pain of the ending has begun.

'The poetry has gone. You're speaking in prose.'

It sounded daft, but I was conveying my sense of our individual sessions. You see, there had always been a poem between us, and the words in themselves were everything, as well as irrelevant. Sometimes we might be composing a lyrical sonnet – no, the sonnet would be composing us – or exchanging meaning in excoriating strips of rap. But always, always, we were crafting a poem.

Now he is lining up language like damp clods of earth. There is nothing of his essence, his spirit, or his passion when we are two people alone. The in-between space resonates with thudding desolation, his interpretations pruned into clipped units. The rhythm of his syntax is shortened. He does not want the poetry of intimacy any more. The pervading texture feels like fear or tension, covered up by distancing. His heart has gone from the work. When I tell him this, his stance is uncompromising. This has got nothing *whatsoever* to do with him. This is *my* history.

I yearn to return to that last individual session before Easter when our relationship had been equal and honest. My hope had been that the final months would sustain that quality of connection. Will he come back to me if I pretend to be an eternal girl – it keeps things safer – as I have done so brilliantly all my life?

You see, when womanhood and sexuality come in, they steal away the people I love.

One day, a glow emanates from J. He is referring to his daughters, in response to something that I have brought into a couch session. But, for the first time, I feel a throat-sadness rising, mingled with crushing disappointment. I do not know how to communicate my feelings when his drawbridge often feels raised these days. Will he bridle up defensively, ever sensing a criticism, which, for once, I do not intend?

'J, I don't want to be treated as a child any more.'

Will he hear this as rejection?

'I don't want to be a daughter by association any more.'

Will he think that I do not appreciate what he offers me, that I am making unreasonable demands, a sure-fire way of antagonising him?

'I want you to see me and meet me as a woman in my own right.'

He does not get it. He seems secure within the old established order.

I am sadly putting on my coat at the end of the session when J makes a throwaway comment – it must have been related to what we had been talking about – that one of his daughters has passed her driving test. In that moment, I realise that she is no longer a child suspended in aspic on the wall, that maybe when J says 'daughter' he is actually thinking of a young woman. There is such envy in me that she is being allowed to grow up, combined with a grief for myself, for what is being denied.

My lifestyle changed in 1996 when I embarked on my first self-employed consultancy. That was when I met Mike, in my eighth summer in therapy.

After Monday's individual session (now at 12.30 p.m.), I would work at home until the group session (now at

6.10 p.m.) and catch the last flight to London. Tuesdays and Wednesdays would be crammed with meetings, and then I would return either last thing on Wednesday night or early on Thursday morning for the second individual session (at 12.15 p.m.). During the August break, I would work in London for a longer period.

Mike was staying at the same halls of residence as me, lecturing on a summer course. He had that look – bespectacled face, comfortable chinos – that conveyed American, middle-class Democrat in his early forties, married with children. The conversation in the canteen was classic two foreigners, trading secrets on the best theatre shows in London.

'Will you be here for breakfast tomorrow?' he asked.

We began to meet. I felt relaxed with him: he was married. We arranged to go out for dinner, and he turned up with a punnet of strawberries, which we ate in the park as an aperitif. We went on to the restaurant, enjoying each other's company. When he walked me back to my room he tried to kiss me. I pulled away, aghast. The delightful time was over.

That night I lay awake. Years of slogging in therapy … supposed to be leaving soon – *upswell of fear* – yet still I was rubbish with men. What had it all been for?

The following evening I saw Mike in the square. I had been thinking about my relationship with J, our human meeting, how he had taught me so much about honesty, about finding a path through insurmountable difficulties to tenderness. It had not been easy, but freedom had started with authentic speaking and listening. I did not want my relationship with Mike to end on the uncomfortable note of the previous evening. I went up to him, 'Could we talk?'

We walked for hours in Regent's Park. He told me what was really going on for him, how he and his wife were at a crossroads. It sounds clichéd. It wasn't. I told him about therapy, my unconscious equivalent. He did not seem fazed: 'Hey, everyone in the States is in therapy.'

It was when we were sitting on a park bench, at 3 a.m., that the conversation became more intimate. He was the first man to talk to me about a woman's power, how a woman was not passive in sex (my internalised image). He said his experience was that a woman actively took a man inside her and how exciting that was for a man. No one had ever told me that about lovemaking, about being a woman. My tummy turned a somersault. Desire was alive in my body – the feeling J often talked about, which I had never understood. I knew how I wanted the night to end.

At 4 a.m., with Mike's flight home in a few hours, we went back to my room and we kissed and explored each other's bodies. I realised that maybe this was why I had denied myself, because my hunger was profound. To be a female sexual being, to not always shut out the possibility of pleasure, to be a woman desiring a man and to trust that a man would not hurt me.

We both knew what he was going to offer: would he help me over the block that had seemingly stalled my life? I wondered was this what I was supposed to do, to say yes to sexual intercourse, to be able to leave therapy, knowing that my oldest terror had been met?

I chose to say no, because I wanted that level of intimacy with a man who would love me and me alone, who would be committed to being with me for many mornings, not just one.

When we exchanged goodbyes, we wished each other the best. He was going to try again with his wife. I was pleased, believing they could work it out. He thought that the man who found me would be lucky indeed.

It was a few weeks before I saw J again. He was in one of those moods where, whenever I hesitated, he would start talking. Eventually I said, 'J, would you ever listen to me?'

And when I told him about what had happened with Mike, he seemed touched.

Letter, undated

J, this is what I think. I think you're not willing to see me as a woman, to share with me the process of ending therapy, to give of yourself in that ending so that I can be free to go. I am not free if you will not properly say goodbye to, and with, me. Can you find it in your heart to embrace the complexity of what has been between us without asking me to betray you, it and myself by constantly referring to it as a great fixation? Why could you only own and name the fixation, not stand up for other real values and meanings? Why could you not respond to what I said with a sharing of yourself? I find it extremely difficult to say goodbye to you, but ending is impossible if we cannot talk mutually about what has been, if we cannot say goodbye *to each other*.

You don't seem willing to meet me in the ending. I don't believe that you don't love me, but I think it makes you afraid. You speak of the grief I have given you, yet you virtually never acknowledge the commitment I gave, whenever I was able. Why are the pain I caused you, the weaknesses I have, easy to comment on, yet you struggle to acknowledge the love I give, not to the world at large, not transference alone, but to you?

It is as if the only language is through dreaming because a dream can just be. I felt angry when I left today and now I feel sad. I can't see the point of going on Monday because I can't keep trying to find some language and way of ending when none seems to be there. You don't want me to express my love for you or to take on board what therapy has truly, madly, deeply meant for me. I may leave, but I can't end. Some months ago you said you had never really seen me as a woman in the therapy. Now I don't think you will ever allow that to be. We crossed a Rubicon together but can't seem to arrive on another shore.

Gary is the group baby, although he is older than me. I am the custodian who remembers the personalities, the altercations and moving-to-tears moments. I have explained to Gary that the group is like a living fossil and the imprints of previous members form part of the stone. Gary comments that he does not want to end up like me: inconsolable. I feel badly about being a poor exemplar for therapy, for J's sake.

Gary asks: '*What* is ending here?'

'Sometimes, it feels like *I'm* ending,' I tell him.

Jeff responds, 'You don't end when the experience ends. It's about making an imaginative leap.'

I know this pitch of anxiety must be connected to early separation from my mother – it feels primitive and primal, yet knowing this with my mind makes no difference. Noel says it is as if the various levels of meaning have telescoped together. It makes him think of the terror of the child, waiting to be born.

Jeff says I want magic resolution, magic certainty and unconditional love.

Eva is disappointed: 'The love doesn't seem to stick to you. It's all externalised, not internalised. A change is required from you too at the ending.'

I feel sick at heart at how the ending of therapy is going. In the stress of the leave-taking, I tell the group I have felt pulled back to the oldest of traumas. Recently, on the couch, I had found myself going over again when the big bomb had exploded and how the gripping thought had been that no one must ever touch me. Yet this time I could let myself feel what I had needed underneath it all, which was for someone to take me in her arms – even if I had gone hysterical – and keep on holding me until the storm was over. And the person I wanted most was my mother.

J leans forward, 'She is asking for Mother's help. Don't leave her with the burden of re-enactment.'

J hesitated, 'Perhaps ... the leave-taking has not been well managed.'

Did some third-party supervisor intervene or did J simply dig deep and self-reflect? For the first time, he seemed open to engaging with the painful feedback that I had been giving him for months, namely that he was energetically gone when we were alone together.

We started to go over the leave-taking sequence. Then I understood why I had felt immediately compelled to give in my notice after J's assertion of love in the group and our subsequent close couch session. Because, once the clock struck midnight, and we saw each other as a man and a woman, like Cinderella I had to flee. Maybe I was replaying an old internalised story, the fear that everything would explode when womanhood and sexuality came in – which it did – so my leave-taking was a protective gesture for others too. But J was also in the room, a real person with his own dynamic around love and intimacy.

It was a conversation of great honesty, after which he assured me, 'Don't worry. The ending has not yet taken place. We still have time.'

'Uncurl your constricted body. Let it assume a position of tranquillity. Take your hands away from your tummy, so that it's not tense. Don't focus downwards, like a serpent feeding on its own tail.'

I lie scrunched up on the couch, sick with that falling-off-a-cliff sensation of fear.

J's calming presence takes effect. 'What is there to be terrified of in the here and now, not the past or the future? We have nowhere to go, nothing to do, other than to be here together.'

The talk is, once more, of difficult separations, first with mother, then turning to father in compensation, then the fall at puberty. The double wound. And here I am again facing separation. On Monday I had told the group how important they had been to me but they did not seem to understand my increasing anxiety.

A childhood memory is stirring: my mother reading me a bedtime story and me desperate to reassure her, 'Don't you know how much I love you and Daddy?' My mother was mystified. 'Yes, of course we do.' Yet my agitation would not cease.

'You were showing her what *you* needed, the reassurance that *you* were loved, that *your* love was known, powerful and seen. Group members were offering you that.'

Only I get so upset I cannot take anything in. I know the group will become exasperated that I cannot hold on to their love. It is as if they have given me water for a desert trek, yet the water keeps leaking through the cracks in my hands.

After last Monday's group session I went back to J's office. He had given me the banana on his desk, his evening tea.

'I wanted to give you something of myself, some nourishment.'

Now J is quoting T.S. Eliot, 'We shall not cease from exploration / And the end of all our exploring / Will be to arrive where we started / And know the place for the first time.' For once, good old T.S. gets it right: how the process of therapy is about knowing the voiceless, nameless place, the ending *is* the beginning, because here we are again at the consciously named hour of early separation.

I talk about trying to resolve demented feelings of fear with my mind, yet my mind reinforces them. J reminds me of psychosynthesis principles.

'You are *more* than your feelings, *more* than your mind. Clouds have more substance than feelings. Bring in Spirit. There is more to you than Ada from *The Piano*. Don't throw yourself off the boat.'

I tell him I had felt downhearted by what he had said about me in the previous group session, how I served war. J denies this. 'I said you did not stand up for love. You are a loving person, have a loving spirit, but you have made the creative, unifying act between two people into an act of terror. You don't have to do this any more. You are brilliant at confronting yourself: what about confronting life? I want to hear an example of you being kind to yourself. You seek this external reassurance, yet your dream imagery shows a need so large that no amount of external reassurance could ever be enough. It is about cultivating *internal* reassurance. Can you nurture in yourself that which is life-affirming? Can you think about what it is that you are willing to stand for and serve? Can you build internal bridges and take hold of life? Because no one else can do it for you.'

After Carmel's death, I would ask J, 'Do you think she's OK, wherever she's gone?' He would rightfully not cross over where it is not for therapy to go. Rather he supported me to fulfil my own destiny, not the one that should have been Carmel's. The years went by; the nightmares lessened; the sadness remained. No one was ever found or jailed for her murder. There was never any explanation for the terrible act.

As the leave-taking grew closer – scheduled for spring 1997 – I came in one day in November 1996, panic-stricken. I told J I had made an awful mistake and should never have given in my notice. I was not ready. I might never be ready. 'Could I stay on?'

J sounded furious – or maybe afraid of being lumbered with me for ever. 'That would be a travesty of the therapy. Give up on the relationship with me. Live with your choice. Grieve with the group.'

That night, I dreamt about Carmel. She appeared in my bedroom, exactly as I remembered her, so alive that I could almost touch her. I was inviting her to go to the cinema with me, to see *To Kill a Mockingbird*. She was delighted, said she would stay the night, sleep on my sofa in a sleeping bag. The dream was lit up with the closeness of a late-night conversation between two old friends. She told me she was feeling much better in herself, and I could see that she was. She talked about the lessons she had learnt since we had last met (I was not sure if she knew that she was dead): about putting people first, about not being introspective, about loving life. She told me she was happy; she radiated it.

I woke up with the numinous comfort of a joyful dream about Carmel. And I heard Carmel telling me 'Go.'

II

Joy

All shall be well,
And all shall be well,
And all manner of thing
Shall be well.

Julian of Norwich

DOES J have a garden? I scan back through hours of conversations. He definitely has a study, because one Christmas I had given him an artist's print, and he had replied, 'Thank you. I will put this in my study.' I remembered my envy since I lived in a small, rented flat. If you have a study, does it follow on that you have a garden? How can I bring the couch sessions around to the information I need?

'J, you know the Gardens of Babylon ...?'

'I've been wondering about the Garden of Eden ...'

The man at the tree nursery has a rugged face. *What a good-looking man,* I catch myself thinking, and am pleased that such a notion can nestle inside me, that I can practise noticing a man in his body and me in mine.

'If it's apple trees you're after, you've come to the right place because we've some beauties.'

The rows of trees are glistening in fledgling green, eager to be assigned good homes. As we wander down muddy paths, I ask, 'Is it true that an apple tree on its own cannot bear fruit?'

'Aye, that's it, and you can cross-fertilise species to produce new scents and tastes.'

J's parting gift had become another vehicle for anxiety. What if the ending went badly in the final session, leaving me relocated in London and desperate to reconnect to him? I would gaze up at the portraits of Sigmund Freud, Carl Jung and Roberto Assagioli, and imagine that they were from a grateful patient. If only I had thought of that.

I had always given J presents. That first Christmas in therapy, when the world was fresh, I watched as cards gathered on his window. So, I thought, cards are allowed. Sometimes I would give a spontaneous offering when a session had gone well and I would feel life expanding with the joy of self-discovery and self-insight, when there had been the pleasure of two people shining light on the obscure reaches of the unconscious, or playing sandcastles with the glorious freedom of free association.

I would need two very different trees, for we are two distinct personalities, yet profoundly alike at the roots. There would be no trace of me in his room – my act of faith in being remembered and going on – yet our work might bear fruit in years to come.

'I promise you,' says the man – and, really, he is *gorgeous* – 'I'll give you the two loveliest trees in the nursery.'

It is a day of couch mellowness, when shared affection can be allowed in after our mutually painful struggle with intimacy. J's voice has a real sense of regret and remorse.

'That time when we were working with the theme of not being special ... I knew what I was trying to do, but I did not work with my heart.'

I think to myself how much J has changed as a therapist, as a human being, that he can acknowledge this aspect of himself, within the honest trust of our long-established relationship. In the honing of the therapeutic art, I realise, forgiveness is required on both sides.

J says, 'I care for you. I love you.'

The room is still.

'I couldn't have said this to you four years ago.' That is so very true. 'I want you to know that you are meaningful to me in a way I tried to deny.'

My heart is touched.

J says a beautiful thing. 'You have been teaching me about therapy.'

How affirming to know that the power is not one-directional, that a patient can give something back, which the therapist can openly appreciate.

'You're more mature now. You don't get wiped out.' He could make the slightest challenging comment, and it might only have been the wind rustling but, to the hypersensitive leaf, it felt like a tornado. 'There is no one else like you.'

I laugh, teasing us both, no longer wanting to take myself terribly seriously, thinking of the hell I have put him through. 'God, isn't that lucky for you!'

It is hard to believe that this love can never be taken away from me, my oldest unconscious terror.

J says, 'I worry about you.'

'Don't. I'll be fine.'

A heart connection warms the room. J speaks again. 'It's difficult for me to say this, to not intellectualise every-thing.'

I think, *Yes, I know.*

'You're such a passionate woman.'

Again I laugh. 'On paper, yeah ...'

He shakes his head, willing to affirm a quality that I find hard to accept is mine.

'No. I've worked with you. You're a deeply passion-ate woman. Yours is a passionate spirit. You're generous, straight and honest. You're not manipulative.'

A man sees and enjoys my passion; it does not have to be deadened. My experience of myself as a woman feels strengthened. J goes on, 'And, yes, I hate bits of you.' This time I hear the gold in the grit. 'I hate what was done to you, what you do to yourself, how you fall into that abyss.' It sounds as if he wants something better for me. 'I hate how you go blind, your negative mirror imaging, the way you feel rejected from my world. I hate how you attack me, de-skill me as a therapist.' De-skilling him has come up as a recent theme. Whatever it means, I want to stop it. 'This isn't about your relationship to your father or mother any more. This is about your relationship to your soul, to the beloved within.'

My heart skips a beat in recognition, even though I have never heard the word 'beloved' used in this context before. With my head it is impossible to understand how you can project soul onto another person; with my heart it is easy.

J is talking about the myth of Psyche and Eros, about the tragic Narcissus who fell in love with his image, not realising that a reflection of the soul and the soul herself are not the same thing. He is veering off in enthusiasm. 'I want you to celebrate your own colour. You've got such a spectrum of colour.'

I feel like a lovely summer rainbow, lighting up the room. I find myself telling J about my friend's new baby.

'I want you to enjoy your *own* husband, to have your *own* babies.'

How many times have I told him that I do not necessarily want a husband or a child – a wee loving relationship would be grand – but the man automatically goes back to his fundamental blueprint of relationships, to what makes him happy. I smile. It really does not matter any more.

'There's lots about you I'd like to change.'

Yes, J, I think I have gathered that.

'I love you, black bits and all.' This is from the man who has experienced the absolute worst in me. I realise I want to reach across and touch his face.

J's voice fills the room, 'I love you just as you are.'

Finally I said it. 'Could our last session be the Thursday before Easter?'

I had been afraid that J would suggest reducing the number of weekly sessions in my last year. He did not. The truth was I could not bear to face any separation. I told myself that I still needed him and the group because there was so much change to be negotiated and because I was like a baby bird preparing for a big flight.

However, this meant that I would be going from over seven years of three sessions a week to no contact at all, in one fell swoop. I often wondered afterwards if my grieving would have been any less if there had been some gentler process of stepping down. It still feels like one of our major mistakes.

J is getting out his diary, looking at the pages ahead. He comments quietly, 'I feel sad you won't be here.'

For the first time, I feel mutual sadness moving between us.

I concentrate on J's every word.

'You have been captured by this vision of a perfect ending, to compensate for what has gone before, but you can't ever get what wasn't given to you in the past. You're away off in the future, rather than being with what *is* in this moment. It's like your father, isn't it, captured by the vision of a dream house, and the vision takes over. Let it go.

'All these years you've been trying to figure out the unfigurable: what was wrong with your love. There was nothing wrong with your love. Your love is crystal pure. You don't have to prove to anyone that you're lovable. *Know* that you're lovable. You're loved by me, and by the group. Really take that in.

'And yes, there's been a tremendous cost. You will get ill again if you don't stay connected to human relationships. You have these high values and ideals. Don't get hijacked by perfectionism and rigidity. You are on a new shore now, leaving the old world behind. Don't go down these dark holes. Don't be like Ada, hanging in the water. *Choose life.*'

The card accompanying one of my last letters had a Picasso painting on it, and J asked if it had any particular meaning for me.

'Oh yes. You see how the baby's sitting on Mother's lap? The baby doesn't need to look up at her mother. The baby can look out at the world. In fact, they're looking in different directions. The baby and her mother know they're secure and bonded. I love that.'

A few days later, I brought in J's amethyst crystal. I told him I had been thinking about how another client might be in trouble some day and might need it. I could go on without it. But – how special to have some tangible reminder of him – J said not to worry, I could keep it.

In one of our last remaining couch sessions, I ask for my biscuit box, which J keeps for me under his office desk. Each session is treasured, knowing that this unique soul intimacy will never come again, no matter how our paths may cross in the future.

Perhaps my box is no longer important, given that my sore heart is much healed. Yet I remember a promise I once made to myself. There is one more task I choose to face.

I ask J, 'Will you hold my hand?'

It was Michael Kearney's book *Mortally Wounded* that prompted the notion: his emphasis on holding a dying person's hand to help them over the threshold. Unfortunately, J does not seem to have read the book because silent unease immediately enters. I, too, regret my request, sensing that I have unintentionally placed J in a difficult position. However, J seems to want to do right by me: he extends his hand. The strangeness of exiled touch, the clamminess of physicality between us, yet we are holding hands at the point of death.

I tip the box's contents onto the floor. It is two years since I made it, and time immemorial since I have been terrorising myself with the knowledge of a bad self. Now I can see everything in the light of day, and so can he. I can stop strangling myself with shaming self-hatred.

The contents seem suffused with pathos. I see the actions of a confused, frightened child who was damaged inside.

J says, 'There is so much more to you than this.'

I know this to be true.

'Will I get rid of it?' he suggests.

Together, we gather up the contents and J steps out of his office. When he returns, the box is gone.

At last, I feel free to go.

J always makes the same comment to Mark in the group. He obliquely refers to the myth of the Gordian knot – I have long given up on steering the man to modernity – then he looks intently at Mark (and he calls me a drama queen!), announcing with a flourish: 'The solution was to slice the knot with a sword.'

I haven't got a clue what he is on about. I don't think Mark is much the wiser either. The myth floats into my mind as I consider a farewell present for Mark. It is a risk – could I find him the sword? Belfast has a distinguished history of supplying Molotov cocktails and Armalite rifles, but swords for the Gordian knot are not the city's speciality. I ring Turkish shops in London (I don't want to malign the Turks, but they might have the odd sword lurking), second-hand shops and antique shops. Nothing. Then Mark announces that he will be away on the evening of my last group, so I will have to give him his present two weeks earlier because of the bank-holiday Monday in between.

I remember the Chinese tradition of sword-fighting and seek out a shop in London where a slight Chinese man eagerly shows me six swords. I lift the first one – too heavy; the second – too large; the third – too sharp. The man murmurs politely, 'Madam, you are buying a sword.' The fourth is light and quick, has a gleam when unsheathed and at its base has an engraved symbol like a dragon. 'Means power, Madam.'

On the evening of my second-last group, I was rushing, so quickly put three items into my shoulder bag: Mark's gift, my accompanying letter for him and a letter I had written to J some months before. J had fulfilled the promise I had asked of him seven years previously and had returned my letters and cards, nearly 200 of them.

As fate would have it, the group's attention turned to Mark, who was feeling low. I listened and thought that when the time was right I would tell him I had a present for him. Then, bang on cue – Oh my God! – J started spouting about the Gordian knot. I wanted to shout triumphantly, 'Not any more, mate!' I let J gambol on.

Finally I turned to Mark. 'I've something for you, but I want to read out my letter to you first, so you'll understand.' I placed the odd-shaped parcel on the floor.

Everyone stared. 'What is it?'

J said, 'It's a sword.'

Drat, the man was clever. I read out Mark's letter – he was thrilled, said the letter alone would have been enough. Then he took the sword out of its exotic box.

J encouraged him, 'Go on, stand up and show us your sword.' It was both funny and serious. Mark stood up and excitedly raised the sword high in the air, like a knight from *Excalibur*.

J admired, 'It suits you.'

And it did. We all agreed. He looked fantastic, a warrior king. No measly Gordian knot was going to beat him now.

It was in this mood that I reached into my bag. 'There's something else I'd like to do. I'd like to read out from a letter I wrote to J several months ago. I called it "Testimony to J".'

Everyone agreed, yes, go on.

I started to read aloud: 'You love with a combination of reserve, passion and integrity. You seek to serve, and you do, yet not with pale, pure colours but with blood and guts and bone.'

The words sounded so intimate in public that I almost lost my nerve. However, I kept going, concentrating on the sincerity of my experience. The letter covered many different aspects of J: what he was like as a therapist, as a person, how he honoured the journey of the soul. For thirty minutes – a third of the entire meeting – there was no sound other than my voice. Finally, I ended by saying that J would always be a part of me, and, if I ever met a man whom I liked, I hoped that I would hear his voice: 'Go for it. Include the fear and risk. Be your truest self.'

For a long time there was no sound other than soul calling out to soul. This was one of those moments when I wanted nothing back, when I loved because I could, because I loved loving, because I had eked out enough confidence to believe that my love as a woman for these two men would be good enough and a larger heart holds us all.

At last J spoke. 'Thank you.'

It was as if he had heard the words for the first time. Yet I had read them out to him ten months previously from the couch, but it was on one of those days when J was like a shiny leaf and the words had bounced off him like rain.

Group members began talking about J's good qualities. I wistfully looked down at my hands and thought, *I'm really leaving.*

They are here, the two men, with their removal van, advance emissaries to usher in my new London career! My last group will be this evening. My final individual session will be on Thursday. The plane taking me to London is on Saturday morning.

As the men pack boxes, I sit in my office, writing. An idea had formed after the last group. I would pen letters of appreciation for each member and read them out while distributing gifts, as I had done with Mark. Now is the moment for expressing love. There is no disputing it, no time to be afraid or shy. I have one last opportunity; I am going to take it.

Should I give J his gift in the group or on his own? After mulling over this dilemma, I have decided to give out everything in the group so that our final couch session will be free of undertakings.

At Christmas – my last Christmas in the group – I had given each member a card and had been disappointed that no one had offered any back. When I had woefully trailed along to the following couch session, J sounded piqued: 'It's an analytic group. It's not about *exchanging Christmas cards.*'

Yes I know, I know. The group is an opportunity to be yourself, to get to learn who that is, in and through relationships with others. It is about belonging to a circle of unremitting honesty, hearing how other people experience you and coming to see how you do indeed create external reality based on an internal world.

I know that. I just wanted one Christmas card to soothe this cavernous anxiety, to reassure me – because in the stress of leave-taking, my core wound has been reactivated – that I would be *remembered*, that I *mattered*, that I was *loved*. So, even though there would be no presents for me, my own giving ritual is important.

Vera's challenge is being seen and heard. I buy her a Maria Callas CD and a tape of Seamus Heaney's poetry, to remind her how glorious the human voice can be.

I associate Jeff with maleness and the sexual. I give him a sculpture based on Teilhard de Chardin's *Love*, two figures embracing.

Noel and I once had a conversation about a region of Ireland that I know well and where he was happy. His gift is a painting of that area.

Gary's gift has to be about encouragement. I am passing the group flame to him, the youngest member. I give him an Irish elm bowl, the oldest symbol of holding.

Eva's journey has been about coming into, and celebrating, the feminine. I give her a silver brooch engraved with a bird and a heart and the phrase 'Loves me, Loves me not.' I thought it would remind her of me.

The presents are wrapped up, like Christmas Day in the middle of March. It is time to put on the red dress I wore to the thank-you party I gave for family, friends and colleagues three weeks ago; giving gratitude is a theme rippling out in all aspects of my life. I feel a bit ridiculous wearing a long dress at 5.30 p.m., but I want to wear something special.

It is a fifteen-minute drive to J's office. I have to figure out how to get the presents up the stairs without being spotted, because surprise is a pleasurable part of any present. If I time it right, people will be leaving the building, so I can sneak through the front door and hide the trees in the ladies' toilets.

It goes to plan. An earlier group of J's emerges with snatches of conversation. Tonight I want to approach them. 'You won't see me here again as I'm leaving therapy. It's immensely happy. I wish you lots of luck.' Of course, I keep my head down to protect our anonymity, yank up my dress and stagger over to the archaic lift, carrying two apple trees and a wicker basket of gifts.

Usually, if you buzz up for the group, you can walk on through. Tonight I want to forewarn J with a knock, in case he is talking to someone or is on the phone.

'Come in.' He is, as ever, in his office lair. He does his own thing until the dot of ten past six when he takes the same seat every week. This is the cue that the group has begun, no matter who else is there.

It is how it was on the first night, with me sitting alone in the circle, nervous, waiting. When J walks over, I think, *the hour has come*. He looks across at me, and his face, which often seems a blank analytic canvas, fills with fondness. His smile is precious to me in this moment, a sweet ray of encouragement on this, our last evening in the group. It says, 'Don't be anxious. Everything will be all right. We are dearest old wayfarers together.'

Earlier that morning, at the outset of my second-last individual session, J had handed me a card from Mark. I had read it aloud to J because I did not want to bundle experiences into separate parcels any more, but to let them flow.

Mark had thanked me for the 'remarkable friendship' I had given him over the years. He said he had witnessed a great change in me and affirmed my integrity and courage in difficult times. He was 'excited at what my romantic life would now become' and wished me every possible success and contentment. 'I know how extraordinary your love is.'

Weeks later, when I was lonely in London, a package arrived from Mark. (I had left my address with J.) In it were two books: Milan Kundera's *Immortality* and Philip Larkin's *A Girl in Winter*, plus Tracy Chapman's *Matters of the Heart* (with a note from Mark, 'My favourite album ever').

We will be seven in the group tonight. People are smiling at me as they enter. I pitch in early, keen to ensure that my task will be fulfilled. 'I have presents for everyone and letters. Could we go round the circle? It won't take long.'

When is it I realise that the giving will not be one-way?

Noel is my first surprise. 'I've got something for you.'

Noel was not in the group the previous week, so he could not have known that I had bought a present for Mark. I am thrilled. It is an anthology: *A Rage for Order: Poetry of the Northern Ireland Troubles.*

'Well, something good had to come out of the Troubles,' he says.

Inside the cover is his inscription: 'Thanks for being you and for all you've given to the group and to me – p. 318, a good poem by Seamus Heaney. With love.' I turn the pages and see that page 318 is from the play *The Cure at Troy.*

I hand him back his book. 'Will you read it for us?'

Noel's voice calls out:

Human beings suffer,
They torture one another,
They get hurt and get hard.
No poem or play or song
Can fully right a wrong
Inflicted and endured.

The innocent in gaols
Beat on their bars together.
A hunger-striker's father
Stands in the graveyard dumb.
The police widow in veils
Faints at the funeral home.

History says, *Don't hope*
On this side of the grave.
But then, once in a lifetime
The longed-for tidal wave
Of justice can rise up,
And hope and history rhyme.

So hope for a great sea-change
On the far side of revenge.
Believe that a further shore
Is reachable from here.
Believe in miracles
And cures and healing wells.

Call miracle self-healing:
The utter, self-revealing
Double-take of feeling.
If there's fire on the mountain
Or lightning and storm
And a god speaks from the sky

That means someone is hearing
The outcry and the birth-cry
Of new life at its term.

What stunning words to celebrate this leave-taking moment, for they include the tragedy of past trauma, mingled with the capacity of life to regenerate itself, to become so much more.

To my even greater surprise, Gary says that he too has something for me – and him new in the group. A ritual is unfolding. I will read out my letter to Gary, give him his present and then – how amazing – he has a letter that he would like to read to me. The group as a whole is witness and participant to the process.

Gary recalls that I was the first person to welcome him into the group. 'Your lovingness is one of your outstanding qualities.' He says being part of my leave-taking process has been a privilege for him, and that I have been an invaluable group mentor. 'Your courage in sharing the depths of your feelings, making yourself vulnerable, trusting yourself and the group I am only beginning to understand as I start to make that journey myself.'

According to him I created a 'spiritual time and place' in the previous session with my willingness to take creative and imaginative risks. 'It was love in action. Your love is powerful and exemplary.' Finally he gives me a CD of Joni Mitchell's *Blue*. 'I chose it because there was something about you that reminded me of the artiste.'

Each person, it emerges, not only has a present for me but also a card or letter. No one meets outside the group. There could not possibly have been any coordination, yet everyone has been inspired to make the same honouring gesture, one outside group convention, like a sea swell of appreciation, rising up in the form that I love.

It is time to let in what I have given to the group and what the group is returning to me.

Jeff's card is an illustration from *Winnie the Pooh*. Christopher, Tigger and Piglet are looking on as Pooh climbs up a tree to catch a kite caught in the branches. The card reads, 'He climbed and he climbed and he climbed.' Inside Jeff had inserted a copy of a pencil caricature of himself and an extract from *The World According to Garp*, 'He knew what every artist should know: as Garp put it, "You only grow by coming to the end of something and by beginning something else. Even if these so-called endings and beginnings are illusions".' Inside the card he has written, 'For your next beginning. My love goes with you.'

His invitation is to trust that there is a heart-love that does not end when either he or I walk out the door. Jeff's present is a sculpture of three figures linked in a dancing circle. How curious, we have each given the other a gift inspired by touch. 'To remind you of the group,' Jeff said.

Vera is next. She is delighted for me and proud of the milestone I have reached. She treasures the memories I am leaving, 'your dreams, insight, love, kindness, honesty and many talents'. She encourages me to 'keep writing', and then gives me her present. 'I hope this will remind you of just how special you are. Go out into the world and enjoy being a special you.'

Her gift is a pretty art-deco china cup and saucer. For years, I will drink peppermint tea from it last thing at night.

Now it is J's turn. The ribbon-festooned trees are ushered in like children dressed up in their First Communion finery and called to do a turn for the relatives. It is then that it dawns on me: how will J get the trees home? There is also a humble accompanying gift: at the last moment I had decided to give him an Irish elm candleholder. I tell him that the hope candle is for him when fear or doubt lures, when he is on the verge of tumbling into his own inner dark pit. Because I know him. He is to light the candle and remember that his loving is powerful, has changed me, and he is never to forget it. After much thought, I have decided to sign his letter 'your loving client,' which seemed both appropriate and accurate.

He listens to my letter, contemplating his hands. He has a copy of the testimony I had read out to the group because he had asked me for it during the intervening week. (How important that he could, at last, take in some goodness for himself, that he could hear feedback through the reactions of the others. 'It was repression of the sublime,' he commented, another concept I recognised from psychosynthesis.)

Touch is rare in this setting. Here you can cry without intervention, not from indifference but out of respect, for such a movement can interrupt that which needs to flow. The only time I have ever seen J touch anyone in the group is when the leave-taker steps back into the world (as I imagine it). Then J shakes their hand, or if the relationship is a long-standing one, puts an arm around the departing shoulder.

In the recent thaw years, I have even seen a hug.

Tonight the form is changing. J is walking across the room, standing in front of me and then, within the yielding body of our group, he leans down and kisses me. He returns to his chair. There is a silence. I think of the group session nearly a year ago when J said that he loved me and I was so shocked that I could not respond. I know what I must do. I stand up, walk across to where he is sitting, lean down and kiss him with all the tender love, gratitude and courage that are within.

The kiss is reciprocal.

Eva is crying. She says, 'What has been happening is beautiful.'

The kiss seems to have lifted some tension, as though we do not have to hold back on this momentous night. Eva is the last one to read aloud her letter. She has spent the weekend looking for a gift for me and has settled on an easy-to-carry pillowcase. 'I imagine you going to bed at night reminded of the love and regard I have for you.'

She says she will sorely miss me. 'You have been such a central part of my own development. I wonder how I will function in the group without you.' She chose her card because she hopes the colours in it reflect 'your vibrancy, insight, imagination, persistence, your aliveness not only to your own feelings, but to other people's. You are gracious and caring.'

She emphasises, 'You will NEVER EVER be forgotten.' Like Vera, she remembers my writing project. 'Please publish. I would love to read your account of the therapeutic journey.' Finally, she has one last message. 'If I have any wish for you it is that you find as many ways as possible to be kind and gentle to yourself. Remember all or as much as you can from what we have said to you. You are dearly loved and highly regarded.'

It is an exquisite night of poetry and presents, tears and laughter, like being round the fire with people who love and accept all of you. These people have been on the receiving end of kicking, railing, flouncing, raging and hating. They have seen me through. I feel like exuberantly reciting my favourite poem, Raymond Carver's 'Late Fragment', so, what the hell, I will.

> And did you get what
> you wanted from this life, even so?
> I did.
> And what did you want?
> To call myself beloved, to feel myself
> beloved on the earth.

J wants to read aloud a poem from my new anthology, James Simmons' 'Lament for a Dead Policeman'. Halfway through he groans, 'I'd forgotten how long this is,' worried in case he is usurping my time. It is fine.

The racked terror about ending therapy is shelving away, replaced by a divine inner peace, the like of which I have never experienced. A mysterious sureness is infusing every cell, as if the in-breath of grace – no other word can describe it – is descending.

It is right to leave the home that is both therapy and Northern Ireland. I must arise and go, fulfil my destiny, which is to love and to be loved.

I choose life.

So many nights I have spent worrying about the ending of therapy, yet the catastrophic fantasy has not happened. Instead, what feels like an epiphany, a spiritual benediction, has come to pass with this most marvellous rite of passage. This is my unimaginable joy come true, when all is well, unbelievably well.

The moment has come when J stands up – for this is the age-old tradition – to initiate the goodbyes. J is not moving. He looks across at me – we are held within this protective circle where there is such an understanding of therapy – and he says, as if it is the indisputable way it is, 'I love you.'

There is no word of hate tonight. All I can think of to reply, to assert my inner confidence, is, 'I know.'

I will lead. I move over to J. We hug each other. It feels normal and loving. Then J steps out of the circle, and I go round, kissing everyone. Some people are crying in this hour of letting go; there are no more tears from me. We members walk down the stairs, one last time. In the car park, Jeff takes my hand. His feels intensely masculine, magnified no doubt by the lack of physical contact between us for years. He gives me one mighty clasp, like he is the channel for a universal energy force propelling me forward. And I know: this has been the most beautiful evening of my life.

It is my last day to go to the room with the couch and the circle. I first came in mid-November 1988, when I was twenty-seven years of age.

Now it is Thursday, 27 March 1997, and I am thirty-six. Perhaps J has become engrossed in the magnificent puzzle that is the human psyche because he is running late ... just when everything had to be perfect. Maybe he is offering one of my prized lunchtime sessions to a new patient, or negotiating with the man who had been mooted to take over my place in the group.

'No one could take your place,' Eva has assured me. 'Yours will always be unique to you.'

As the minutes tick by, no matter how much work I have done, I feel that slide into the earliest sense of not being held. My fear that everything will go wrong at the very last moment is materialising. Eventually, the waiting-room door opens. My nervousness has increased ten-thousandfold.

I perch on the edge of the couch, disappointed. Will our last session drift away in a welter of sorting out? J says he is sorry. We talk a little. My heart settles.

J rallies, 'Will we make the most of the time we have left?'

We can dwell on the last important matters concerning the existential meaning of life.

I quip, 'OK. Do you have a garden?'

Thank God, he does. He says he will plant the trees in pots outside his home. I smile to myself, thinking how, in imagination, I wanted them to produce a wild orchard. The room permeates with fond reminiscence: do you remember when ...?

Then J says: 'We've been to hell and back.' This is true.

'Well, will you join me in a glass of champagne?'

I cannot stop laughing. J goes over to the baby fridge behind his desk, produces a proper bottle of chilled champagne and two glasses, which he sets down on the floor, like an idyllic picnic on the hottest of summer days. It is the most wonderful gesture – unconventional, funny and beautiful. Sigmund, Carl and Roberto stare on, disbelieving, yet willing to be bemused. Only Mrs Klein adopts a disapproving air.

I silently plead, 'Mel, I fought for you once. Allow me this special moment.'

J cracks open the bottle – pop! – pours out two frothy glassfuls and hands one to me.

We raise glasses to each other in a gleeful toast. 'Here's to us! Here's to our work together! Haven't we just been brilliant?!'

Bibliography

Assagioli, R. (1974) *The Act of Will: A Guide to Self-Actualisation and Self-Realisation*, Harmondsworth: Penguin.

—— (1975) *Psychosynthesis: A Manual of Principles and Techniques*, London: Turnstone.

Barnes, B., S. Ernst and K. Hyde (1999) *An Introduction to Groupwork: A Group Analytic Perspective*, Basingstoke: Palgrave Macmillan.

Campbell, J. (1953) *The Hero with a Thousand Faces*, New York: Pantheon.

Cardinal, M. (1993) *The Words to Say It: An Autobiographical Novel*, trans. Pat Goodheart, London: The Women's Press.

Dinnage, R. (1989) *One to One: Experiences of Psychotherapy*, London: Penguin.

Ferrucci, P. (1989) *What We May Be: The Vision and Techniques of Psychosynthesis*, 2nd edn, Wellingborough: Crucible Press.

Foulkes, S.H. (c. 1964) *Therapeutic Group Analysis*, New York: International Universities Press.

Gray, Miranda (2009), *Red Moon*, Peterborough: Upfront.

Gunn, G. (2002) *Wool-Gathering or How I Ended Analysis*, London: Brunner-Routledge.

Herman, N. (1999) *Sister Mary: A Story of a Healing Relationship*, London: Whurr.

Hillman, J. (1972) *The Myth of Analysis: Three Essays in Archetypal Psychology*, Evanston, Ill.: Northwestern University Press.

Houston, J. (1987) *The Search for the Beloved: Journeys in Mythology and Sacred Psychology*, Los Angeles, Calif.: Tarcher.

Jacoby, M. (1984) *The Analytic Encounter: Transference and Human Relationship*, Toronto: Inner City.

Jung, C.G. (1983) *Memories, Dreams, Reflections*, recorded and edited by Angela Jaffé, trans. Richard and Clara Winston, London: Fontana Press. First published 1963.

Kahn, M. (1997) *Between Therapist and Client: The New Relationship*, rev. edn, New York: Owl.

Kearney, M. (1996) *Mortally Wounded: Stories of Soul Pain, Death and Healing*, Dublin: Marino Books.

Knight, L. (1986) *Talking to a Stranger: A Consumer's Guide to Therapy*, London: Fontana.

Malcolm, J. (2004) *Psychoanalysis: The Impossible Profession*, London: Granta.

Mitchell, S.A. (1993) *Hope and Dread in Psychoanalysis*, New York: Basic Books.

Storr, A. (2001) *Freud: A Very Short Introduction*, Oxford: Oxford University Press.

Symington, N. (1986) *The Analytic Experience: Lectures from the Tavistock*, New York: St Martin's Press.

Tiberghien, S.M. (1995) *Looking for Gold: A Year in Jungian Analysis*, Einsiedeln: Daimon.

Woodman, M. (1985) *The Pregnant Virgin: A Process of Psychological Transformation*, Toronto: Inner City.

Yalom, I. (1991) *Love's Executioner and Other Tales of Psychotherapy*, London: Penguin.

—— (2001) *The Gift of Therapy: Reflections on Being a Therapist*, London: Piatkus.

Yalom, I. with M. Leszcz (2005) *The Theory and Practice of Group Psychotherapy*, 5th edn, New York: Basic Books.

Young-Eisendrath, P. and M. Miller (2000) *The Psychology of Mature Spirituality, Integrity, Wisdom, Transcendence*, London and New York: Routledge.

Acknowledgements

THIS BOOK would not have been possible without the love, faith, support and encouragement of many people, especially my friends, family and colleagues. Thank you all.

There are some individuals whom I need to name.

First, I wish to thank 'J' for agreeing that I could publish this story. I have not named you, J, but I hope that this book stands as a tribute to you and to our work together.

I wish to thank the group members. I was not able to consult with everyone; however, in the final months before publication, I happened to meet one of the group members. I would like to thank her for taking the time to read the draft and to give me her feedback. I hope my depiction gives a sense of the group experience, without revealing the identity of any individual members, or breaking confidentiality.

To Call Myself Beloved would not have come to fruition without the loving sustenance and guidance of my three trusted readers: Jane Clarke, Shirley McClure and Nuala Patterson.

Two places provided me with wonderful sanctuary to write: the Natura Beach Hotel in Polis, Cyprus and The Tyrone Guthrie Centre at Annaghmakerrig, County Monaghan. I would also like to acknowledge The British Library in London and Turvey Abbey in Bedfordshire.

Four influential teachers taught me about psychotherapy, spirituality and womanhood, and to them I am deeply indebted: Miceál O'Regan, Jarlath F. Benson, Helena Løvendal-Duffell and Olivia Russell.

My studies at the Institute of Psychosynthesis in London made a great impact on my writing. I would like to thank my Year Group, my Applied Group, all my trainers and supervisors, with particular acknowledgement to the Institute's founders, Joan and Roger Evans.

I also wish to pay tribute to the Women's Group where I received support with the challenge of writing. Thanks to Inga Bachmann, Debra Bourne, Penny Graham, Susan Green, Ana Kirby, Jane Lamb and Christine Nutt.

Four professionals played an important role on the road to publication: Liz Hudson, Eric King, Julia McCutchen and Christina Rodenbeck.

Others who made a valued contribution include: Valerie Adams, Sue Booth-Forbes, Emma Philbin Bowman, Nina Davies, Dorry Ender, Tess Gallagher, Marina Hughes, Geoff Lamb, Majella McCullagh, Philomena O'Donnell, Joan O'Donovan, Sheila Pratschke, Maureen Schild, John Sutton and my Annaghmakerrig friends.

The literary agent Jonathan Williams was the midwife who expertly guided this work into the world. It has been an absolute privilege and pleasure working with him; his faith kept my book alive.

My warmest thanks are due to everyone at New Island Books, particularly Eoin Purcell.

Finally, I owe the deepest gratitude to my mother. I spoke to her about my manuscript at a time when my father was ill. She gave me her backing to go ahead and seek a publisher, in the hope that my book might help another and also give me pleasure as a creative act. I wish to honour and thank my mother with all my heart for her love and generosity of spirit.

Permission Notes

The author and publisher would like to thank the copyright holders for permission to reproduce the following material.

Rumi, 'A Man and a Woman Arguing', from *The Essential Rumi*, translated by Coleman Barks with John Moyne, A. J. Arberry, and Reynold Nicholson, London: Penguin, 1999. Reprinted with the kind permission of Coleman Barks.

'I Am Not I', by Juan Ramón Jiménez, from *Lorca and Jiménez: Selected Poems*, chosen, translated, and with a preface by Robert Bly, Boston, Mass.: Beacon Press, c. 1997. Translation copyright © 1973, 1997 by Robert Bly. Reprinted by permission of Georges Borchardt, Inc., for Robert Bly.

Galway Kinnell, 'Saint Francis and the Sow', in *Three Books: Body Rags: Mortal Acts, Mortal Words: the Past*, Boston, Mass.: Houghton Mifflin, 1993. Reprinted by permission of Houghton Mifflin Harcourt.

e.e. cummings, 'i thank You God for most this amazing'. Copyright 1950, (c) 1978, 1991 by the Trustees for the E. E. Cummings Trust. Copyright (c) 1979 by George James Firmage, from *E. E. Cummings: Complete Poems: 1904–1962*, edited by George J. Firmage. Used by permission of Liveright Publishing Corporation.

Seamus Heaney, *The Cure at Troy: A Version of Sophocles' Philoctetes*, London: Faber and Faber, 1991. Reprinted by permission of Faber and Faber Ltd.

Raymond Carver, *Late Fragment* by Raymond Carver. Copyright © 1996, Tess Gallagher, used by permission of The Wylie Agency (UK) Limited from *All of Us* by Raymond Carver. Published by Harvill Press. Reprinted by permission of the Random House Group Limited.

T.S. Eliot, 'Little Gidding', *Four Quartets*, London: Faber, 1995, c. 1979. Reprinted by permission of Faber and Faber Ltd.

All reasonable efforts have been made to identify and contact copyright holders. If you hold or administer rights for materials published here, please contact us. Any errors or omissions will be corrected in subsequent editions.